I0796513

FLOWERING OUTDOORS

FLOWERING OUTDOORS

Gardens & Parties

MARGOT SHAW

EDITOR-IN-CHIEF OF *FLOWER* MAGAZINE

WITH LYDIA SOMERVILLE

DESIGN BY ELLEN SHANKS PADGETT

FOREWORD BY BUNNY WILLIAMS

New York · Paris · London · Milan

DEDICATION

In view of my worldview that it all began in a garden, I dedicate this book to the Master Gardener.

CONTENTS

FOREWORD

Bunny Williams
Falls Village, Connecticut

From the first issue I ever received of *Flower* magazine, I knew I had found a soulmate in Margot Shaw. We share a passion for flowers, gardens, home, and entertaining, and in her new book, *Flowering Outdoors*, she shows not only how to live in a garden but how to entertain in the garden. You get to wander from one beautiful garden to another, some with entertaining spaces and others just for strolling, but always with a place to rest and take in the beauty. You can almost hear the birds in each one. The gardens are unique, each with inspiring details.

Shaw has chosen some of the greatest style icons to show how they entertain in their gardens or on a nearby loggia. The beautiful tables filled with flowers or fruits from the garden are set with artistry and make you long to be invited to one of those gatherings. Page after page will give the reader a feast for the eyes as well as ideas to try for themselves.

Although I have many, many books, this is one I am adding to my collection since I never tire of looking at inspirational images of gardens and tablescapes, which encourage me to be more creative.

—*Bunny Williams*

Bunny in the garden of her country home in Connecticut.

INTRODUCTION

Margot Shaw
Birmingham, Alabama

I have always been an early riser. Not that I am particularly industrious, wanting to get a jump on the day per se. I just love daylight. And I believe it is mostly because I love light. Natural light. Light that illuminates the male cardinal I look for every morning—and he often appears. Light that nourishes and highlights what has bloomed in the garden my husband so lovingly tends—I awoke a few weeks ago to a full-blooming tulip magnolia where there had been but branches and buds the day before—the play of light and shadow making it even more graphic and sculptural. As I strolled in the garden I was treated to a showy swath of forsythia, newly blooming, but as if that were not enough, it was backlit.

I love how the sun shifts through the year, lighting the same evergreens in different ways, like they have had costume changes with the seasons. Not everyone is as light obsessed as I. I recall the first time my husband and I went for a trail ride on our farm. He stopped his horse and pointed to a deer scrape on a tree. I then stopped my horse and remarked on the dappling of the sunlight on the leaves of that same tree. Our life together, on the farm and beyond, has continued in that vein. He directs my attention to the wonders of the natural world, and I turn his attention to the play of light that enables us to see them.

When inspired to embark on this book, one that would focus on outdoor living with a floral accent, it came to me that it would be fitting, as some of the most magical moments and discoveries in my cultural canon have been set in the out of doors: Think Manet's *Déjeuner sur l'Herbe*; or the works of the Luminists; the magnificent gardens of Versailles (which to a seven-year-old on my first visit seemed like something from another, unimaginable world—and really still do); the giant Albert Bierstadt painting I sit and ponder from time to time at our local museum; the light on the ocean in the opening scene of the film version of *Persuasion* with the strains of Chopin mimicking the twinkling sun; me, as a little girl, discovering my love of horses, especially cantering across gorgeous green fields dotted with stands of black-eyed Susans in the Alabama countryside; all the way to my foray outside this morning after a violent wind and thunderstorm in the night as I marveled that no trees were down and not a hellebore was bruised, then turning to soak in the surreal sunlit blue-gray clouds that only appear after a storm. Almost worth the storm.

When culling material for this book, I selected a few nighttime projects. They were pretty. But in the end, I found that I could not bear to sacrifice the real estate, and thus all the outdoor living florally in these pages happens in the glorious light of day. All the better to see the flowers.

Come along with me to celebrate at parties imbued with flowers and stroll through some gorgeous gardens.

Margot on the front porch of her Birmingham house.

GARDEN PARTIES

Summer in Style

Kate Rheinstein Brodsky
East Hampton, New York

Kate Rheinstein Brodsky keeps a packed calendar for three-quarters of the year, but when the weather starts to warm up, life slows down a bit—especially when she arrives at her home in East Hampton. "Time seems to stand still a little longer here," said the wife, mother of three tween daughters, and founder of KRB, her eponymous boutique featuring impeccably curated antiques, vintage, and one-of-a-kind furniture, art, and accessories. "It is a much-needed change of pace." Brodsky knows firsthand about living life in the fast lane. The Los Angeles native moved to New York City to attend New York University and then completed stints with Jeffrey Bilhuber, Ralph Lauren Home, and *Elle Decor* before setting up shop just a few blocks from her prewar apartment on Manhattan's Upper East Side.

Needing an escape from the city, she and husband Alexander purchased their circa 1901 home after years of searching for the perfect location. The house, situated on almost an acre near the beach, is just a few blocks from the homes of several family members. When they get away, they can do so in good company. In fact, Brodsky says that one of her favorite things about retreating to East Hampton during the summer is having the opportunity to gather with family and friends outdoors.

"Growing up in California, we lived a very 'alfresco' lifestyle," she says. "I wanted to replicate that here since that is not very doable in the city. When we embarked on our extensive renovation, I was intent on having a variety of outdoor 'rooms' that serve different functions just like interior rooms do," she says. "I was also firmly against adding any other structures on the property. I love that our house is old, wonky, and a little quirky. Anything too new or big would have taken away from that."

With that mindset, Brodsky worked with Bories & Shearron Architecture to create a seasonal pool "tent" in lieu of a permanent pool house. Roughly fifteen by nine feet in size, it consists of an all-weather awning that ties to a metal frame so that it can be deconstructed and stored during the winter months. In true California fashion, the tent is every bit as comfortable for lounging as an interior room would be, and its appointments are just as chic.

For a dining space, the architects dreamed up a pavilion featuring an allée of plane trees trained with bamboo rods to forge a canopy. A slender Fermob bistro table paired with French-inspired folding chairs

A minibar is set up on scalloped metal consoles by Reed Smythe. The hue of the tables is the same eighteenth-century shade chosen by Dolley and James Madison for the shutters at Montpelier. Annabelle hydrangeas straight from the garden are corralled in an amber glass leech bowl designed by homeowner Kate Rheinstein Brodsky and handblown by local artisans exclusively for her shop, KRB.

TONIC WATER
PLYMOUTH
MONKEY 47

stands atop the gravel floor, giving off a very Euro-Cali vibe. "A 'dining pavilion' sounds so glamorous, doesn't it?" says Brodsky. "I have to have a little glam; after all, I am from Los Angeles." She quickly adds, "We do not take ourselves too seriously, though," continuing "the dinner parties we host usually include something simple like a fresh salad, some roasted vegetables, or even takeout. As I say to my husband, I can cook, but sometimes I just choose not to. Besides, if you spread out an embroidered tablecloth and bring out festive colored plates and glassware, no one will think twice about who cooked the food."

ABOVE AND BELOW: "It is like an addiction—I just cannot stop collecting anything and everything for the table," says Brodsky, who discovered her passion for collecting at age six with miniature watering cans. BELOW, FROM LEFT: Freshly clipped zinnias and other flowers from the garden sit on a tray from the Lacquer Company. In a clever nod to the coastal environs, Brodsky serves oysters in a clamshell bowl. OPPOSITE: Architects Richard Bories and James Shearron designed the tent to serve as a temporary pool house that packs away during the colder seasons. Appointed in varying shades of green, it blends with the lush landscape. FOLLOWING SPREAD: A bubblegum pink embroidered tablecloth by Carolina Irving & Daughters and magenta antique French damask napkins from Guinevere Antiques pack some punch into the layers of green in the dining pavilion. In lieu of a matching dining set, Brodsky paired a Fermob table with metal folding chairs by Terrain. The chair frames recall the iconic late nineteeth-century style but feature deeper seats for modern comfort.

BRODSKY'S OUTDOOR ENTERTAINING ESSENTIALS

- A lively, interesting centerpiece: Fresh flowers on a table are lovely, but a potted begonia stripped of its petals is much more intriguing. I also think an artful arrangement of fruits or vegetables keeps things interesting. There is nothing more fabulous looking than Romanesco.
- Glass hurricanes: In addition to being pretty, they are practical on breezy nights when candles are prone to blowing out. I hoard nineteenth-century American glass, and I based my KRB hurricane off an extra curvy one I have in my own collection.
- Cloth napkins: I do not do paper; however, I am not above using a good-looking dish towel as a napkin if the meal is messy. Some of my favorite cloth napkins come from Houses & Parties. They have a great selection in various sizes and styles.
- A minibar: Not the kind you are thinking of, but a little bar set up outside so guests—or hosts—are not traipsing back and forth to the house for refills. We always have wine, sparkling water, and a cocktail option or two. My husband is partial to gin and tonic, which feels very summery, so we generally have the makings for that.
- Takeout: Put some premade goodies on a gorgeous plate. It is just that easy. Shucked oysters from your local seafood market are delicious and feel festive when displayed with all the accoutrements. Even chips and dip somehow seem special when you put them in an antique bowl set on a lacquer tray.

ABOVE: Brodsky's early twentieth-century shingle-style house is located near the beach in East Hampton. PREVIOUS SPREAD AND OPPOSITE: Colorful linens and glassware, including Brodsky's bespoke handblown hurricanes, adorn the dining table. Big, bold zinnias are contained in ceramic vases resembling tin cans sourced from Bloom in nearby Sag Harbor.

On the Rocks

Anne Hamilton
Newport, Rhode Island

When Matt Hamilton was a boy growing up in Philadelphia, he spent idyllic summers in Newport, Rhode Island, with his family and a constant rotation of guests. With such indelible memories of those carefree years, Hamilton could not wait for his own children to have those same experiences. "I have been coming to Newport for sixty-seven years," he says. "My wife Anne and I are the third generation that has spent summers here. All four of our sons have places here, and our daughter and family live on the island full-time."

In the early years of their marriage, the Hamiltons vacationed in different places on his parents' property. But when a friend mentioned that a home abutting Hammersmith Farm, where Jackie Kennedy spent much of her childhood, might be for sale, the couple took notice. "We always wanted a house on the water," says Matt. "I had passed this one a million times on my boat and never paid much attention to it. But when Anne and I took an intentional look at it, we agreed it was special. It has the best views in Newport, including the Newport Bridge, Jamestown, and historic Fort Adams." The Hamiltons bought the property the next day and aptly named it "On the Rocks."

As the couple spent the next few years entertaining friends and hosting various benefits for favorite local nonprofits—including Newport Hospital, Newport Historical Society, Boys and Girls Clubs of Newport County, and the Newport Show, an antiques show that Anne founded and has run for the past fifteen years—they realized that their existing outdoor gathering spaces needed an overhaul to better accommodate large groups. They also wanted to upgrade the recreational facilities for their children and grandchildren to enjoy. To tackle the project, the Hamiltons contacted Hoerr Schaudt, a Chicago-based architectural landscape firm whose work they admired. "Then, because we believe in supporting local businesses, we hired Middletown builder Kirby Perkins, whom I had known when we were kids," says Matt.

Water views from the Hamilton's Newport home are best enjoyed from Adirondack chairs perched on the edge of the property.

This dream team began by reconfiguring the terrace to make it more user-friendly with the addition of spacious cooking, dining, and sitting areas around two matching fireplaces. A long pergola covers part of the space, providing a sense of separation and a bit of shade. "It becomes an additional house with no walls that has a modern feel," says Nick Fobes of Hoerr Schaudt. With permission from the Coastal Resources Management Council, the design professionals also refashioned the outdated heart-shaped pool into a sleek, heated infinity pool whose color blends with the bay.

The surrounding landscape is appropriately embraced by hundreds of native white hydrangeas, lilacs, and waving ornamental grasses. "This project could not have worked out more perfectly," says Anne. "At first I thought I wanted a formal garden, but Doug Hoerr reminded me that the ocean is my garden." Now she finds herself taking in the view every chance she gets. As she says, "We use the space much more than we ever imagined."

ABOVE: Anne Hamilton economizes her efforts by creating floral arrangements that can adorn the Saturday night table for supper with visitors and a luncheon the next day with her friends. BELOW: Sectional seating affords a spectacular ocean view. OPPOSITE: Tabletop decor includes charming dinnerware by Haviland & Parlon, paired with delicate Fern stemware by William Yeoward, Tahiti periwinkle napkins, and Dahlia napkin rings. She created low-lying, lush arrangements of roses, ranunculus, and sea holly to allow for easy conversation over the centerpieces. Narrow table lamps bring in some height at either end of the table. FOLLOWING SPREAD: The collaboration of homeowners and designers resulted in a refined melding of land and sea, house and pool that visually underscores the Hamilton's respect for this fragile coast, as well as the team's determination to preserve it.

HAMILTON'S HINTS FOR OUTDOOR ENTERTAINING

- Never be too timid to use fine china and crystal outside. The natural beauty of the outdoors plays perfect host to a sophisticated celebration.
- For this gathering, napkins with a periwinkle border complement the blues of the seat cushions—fitting for this maritime locale. Simple ranunculus, seeded eucalyptus, and cosmos in Yeoward vases complete the setting.
- Make the most of your entertaining efforts with back-to-back parties. After hosting ten friends for the Saturday evening dinner party, we followed up with a Sunday brunch for my Newport girl pals.

Southern Hospitality on the North Shore of Long Island

Meg Braff
Long Island, NY

Early summer evenings beg for alfresco dinners. And when the soirée is set on the North Shore of Long Island and hosted by interior designer Meg Braff, then prepare for party perfection. Braff grew up in Tupelo, Mississippi, a place where entertaining was and is considered an art form. "My mother would prepare food for days, and on the night of the party, I would help set the table and then get dressed up and 'pass the rolls.' It was my official job," says Braff.

With the rhythms of life so different today, Braff wisely plans a simple but delicious menu when she entertains. Taking a cue from great Southern entertainers including her mother, Braff crafts a menu of comfortable, familiar flavors presented elegantly. For this summer gathering, she chose a light menu of a green salad, chicken breast with fresh vegetables, and pavlova with peaches for dessert.

The afternoon of the party, she spent time in front of the china cabinets, musing over stacks and stacks of plates. "My mother and grandmother instilled in me a love of fine china, linens, and the art of setting the table. They are certainly the root of my china-hoarding tendencies," Braff confesses. Her inspiration was a classic Tassinari & Chatel floral fabric tablecloth in summer bright colors. She picked up the vibrant green in the tablecloth in vintage lily pad plates by Jean Roger and oversize lettuce leaf–form water glasses.

Her abundant gardens yielded the lion's share of the flowers for table decoration and throughout the house. Braff's trusted friend and team member Jason Schwartz artfully mixed them with selections from the flower market in New York City. On arrival, guests were offered a refreshing seasonal cocktail—a passion fruit margarita garnished with edible flowers and sprigs of mint—with replenishment available from a festive bar cart out on the patio. One of those guests, Braff's mother, sat enjoying the shimmer of a party beautifully planned and executed. She wore a glowy, loving look of approval and pride, as well she should.

Meg Braff and a friend collaborated on the table settings from her extensive collection. The floral centerpieces echo the colors in the vibrant tablecloth made from a heritage French fabric line.

ABOVE: Guests served themselves from this smartly dressed bar cart. OPPOSITE, CLOCKWISE FROM TOP LEFT: The hostess, dressed in a joyous poppy-colored maxi dress, carries arrangements to the dinner table. Party guests mingle before dinner.

BELOW: A soft perennial border yields many a bloom for party arrangements. OPPOSITE, CLOCKWISE FROM TOP LEFT: The chinoiserie monogrammed napkins are from Julian Mejia Design. A goblet doubles as a vase for an informal bouquet of lady's mantle, spray roses, and chamomile. Retro-latticework lowball glasses add another outdoor design element to the decor. To hold the centerpiece of peonies, lady's mantle, delphinium, chamomile, and lilac, Braff chose her Vladimir Kanevsky porcelain cabbage tureen.

BRAFF'S GUIDE TO GETTING HER LOOK

- Embrace color: Braff prefers cheerful, uplifting palettes that reflect her surroundings and remind her of places she loves. Her personal penchant for blues and greens reflects her affinity for beach and tropical locations.
- Buy things you love: Mixing new items with storied objects creates an extra layer of interest. Sometimes, it's the one-of-a-kind items that set the tone for a whole room. Braff's fondness for chinoiserie, bamboo, and Chinese-inspired fabrics comes from her love of travel to Asia.
- Cherish heirlooms: Family pieces tell stories of your heritage. Some of Braff's favorites include her grandmother's bed that she inherited as a teenager and a grand dining table that seats eighteen at her family's Mississippi lake house.

ABOVE: A boxwood garden flanks the entrance to Braff's Locust Valley house. OPPOSITE, CLOCKWISE FROM TOP LEFT: A topiary boxwood nestles in a pillow of white blooms. Braff's peonies thrive in profusion. "There's a view of the garden from every room in the house," says Braff. One such focal point features a Zen-like gravel courtyard centered on a fountain. Irises and salvia play off yellow and green tones in a deep border.

Gaming in the Garden

Mary Hollis Huddleston and Katie Jacobs
Nashville, Tennessee

Mah-jongg is making a comeback. Grounded in tradition, the game has historically been associated with older generations. However, thanks to its inherent social nature that encourages community, often over food and drinks, mah-jongg has become the "it" game for all ages. It also creates a great excuse for throwing a party.

When Nashville stylist and party planner, Mary Hollis Huddleston, received her first set of custom Kelly-green mah-jongg tiles, she immediately called upon her dear friend and fellow entertaining expert, Katie Jacobs, to help host an afternoon of food and festivities centered around the chic pastime. Huddleston and Jacobs have both made careers out of entertaining and styling tables. Since Jacobs is a wizard in the kitchen, she is also willing to handle the menu.

Jacobs also has the gift of a green thumb, and her colorful garden just outside of Nashville provided the most enchanting setting for their gathering. "This garden is a family project," she says. "My husband and I, along with our children, tend to it every day. It now consists of multiple raised beds, including two flower beds and two herb beds, as well as an in-ground growing area." Using the garden as the setting for a gathering is not new to Jacobs. As an author, stylist, and photographer, she has used the space to host numerous dinners, celebrations, and photo shoots.

To set the game table, Huddleston selected a decorative game-table topper with a scalloped brushstroke green pattern to complement the mah-jongg tiles. She procured hand-embroidered cocktail napkins, along with an assortment of playful acrylic mah-jongg stir sticks for the beverages. The duo set up a wicker drinks table to hold lavender glassware along with several mouthwatering snacks and beverages courtesy of Jacobs.

"Summer is my absolute favorite time to invent new recipes inspired by what comes out of the garden that day," says Jacobs. "For this party, I focused on pops of color with simple fresh bites that are easy to eat while playing table games." Guests happily passed around plates of crostini topped with golden beets, arugula, goat cheese, edible flowers, and tomato, along with charred corn and ricotta with fresh basil.

For the dining table setting, Huddleston played off the colors in Jacobs's garden using a floral tablecloth. She also brought in her personal collection of hand-painted Ginori plates to complement the pink accents in the mah-jongg tiles. "When setting an outdoor table, I love using as many natural elements as possible, so I chose bamboo-handle flatware, as well as woven chargers and napkin rings," she says.

Flowers are always a necessity for her table settings, but they were even more important in this lush garden setting. While Jacobs and Huddleston both

Guests dined at Katie Jacobs's stone table nestled in the midst of her vibrant garden. For the table setting, Mary Hollis Huddleston drew inspiration from the abundance of flowers in Jacobs's garden.

enjoy arranging their own flowers, they also believe in delegation, so they enlisted friends from the Tulip Tree to help. Using fresh blooms plucked on-site, they created arrangements of sunflowers, zinnias, cosmos, dahlias, poppies, Queen Anne's Lace, and globe amaranth.

No party is complete without favors—and Jacobs and Huddleston knew theirs would come in handy during the party, so they did not wait until the end to hand them out. The woven, handheld fans from Klatso Home helped guests keep cool in the Southern heat. And as the game came to a close and players began to say their goodbyes, each guest took home the keepsake as a reminder of the special occasion.

ABOVE: Hudldleston and Jacobs collaborated on creating an elevated mah-jongg experience. BELOW, LEFT TO RIGHT: Mah-jongg tile stir sticks from Acrylic Sticks were clustered together in a small terra-cotta pot. Guests enjoyed two variations of crostini: beet, arugula, and goat cheese with edible flowers and tomato, charred corn, and ricotta cheese with fresh basil. OPPOSITE: Jacobs served up her famous lemon and white chocolate chip cookies with lavender on a vintage mint-green cake stand. Flowers from Jacobs's garden formed an exuberant arrangement. FOLLOWING SPREAD: The table setting played off the colors in Jacobs's garden using a floral tablecloth and placemats. Hand-painted Ginori plates were chosen to complement the pink accents in the mah-jongg tiles.

Amy

HUDDLESTON & JACOBS'S MODERN-DAY MAH-JONGG OUTSIDE

- For a party centered on game play, it is smart to serve finger food that is easy to eat, like deviled eggs topped with caviar.
- Natural materials are suitable for the garden setting. Woven place mats, caned cup holders, and a rattan bar cart all bring a casual vibe to the festive setting.
- Many mah-jongg tiles feature floral designs, which are reflected in the vibrant floral arrangement.
- Chargeable table lamps are a great investment and cast the prettiest light when the sun goes down.
- Woven handheld fans served a purpose in the steamy Nashville weather and also went home with guests as souvenirs.

ABOVE: Colorful tiles from The Mahjong Line complemented the green-striped topper from Fenwick Fields. To provide ample room for game play, Huddleston set up a separate drinks table that was easily accessible to guests. OPPOSITE, CLOCKWISE FROM TOP LEFT: Pretty paper shades on chargeable table lights echoed the colors of the place settings. Doubling as a work of art, Jacobs's kiwi cheesecake topped with edible flowers was served on a wicker cake stand from Amanda Lindroth. Woven, handheld fans kept guests cool and also served as party favors. Game table beverages, including a delightful strawberry thyme lemonade, were served in lupine-colored Rialto glasses.

Aglow in the Allée

Frances Schultz
Santa Ynez Valley, California

Writer, style icon, and proud Southerner, Frances Schultz could legitimately be called a grande dame, save for the fact that she exudes a warm and welcoming energy. As a North Carolinian transplanted to Southern California by way of New York City, her Southern hospitality gene has if anything grown stronger.

"Being lucky to land in the middle of the postcard-pretty Santa Ynez Valley, a stone's throw north of Santa Barbara, we lived on a ranch seemingly designed for entertaining. And entertain we have," she says. "From improvised opera nights and ersatz cabarets to rootin' tootin' rodeos and storybook weddings, our Rancho La Zaca has seen it all. But at the end of the day, nothing beats just having a few friends to dinner." In the cathedral-like allée of olive trees, Schultz loves to set a table for an intimate dinner where the day's last light filters through the branches and the sunset floats in an endless sky.

Schultz is, at heart, a pragmatist, and as such approaches entertaining with a gimlet eye. "As much fun as it is to decide to have a party, however, there invariably arrives that tiny spasm between delight and dread when one must figure out exactly what and how one will arrange it all, and how to make it memorable."

Schultz takes a painterly approach to composing a table setting. "With our table planned around our region's always-bountiful harvest, the farmers market is as inspiring as the flower shop," she says. "As an amateur artist, I also love thinking in terms not just of floral centerpieces but of still life scenes

The bar makes a good focal point, as guests invariably congregate there. In creating a table, author, artist, and host Frances Schultz thinks in terms of a tableau, composing elements as she might in a still life to paint.

that are dynamic and varied in terms of subject, color, and texture. In the world of paintable fruits, melons are right up there, and nothing says summer like watermelon: sweet, juicy, thirst-quenching happiness. Green grapes from our vineyard on a runner of sheet moss emphasized the red-and-green complement of the melons, and the flowers carried through in softer shades of coral, pink, and orange, with olive foliage clipped from the canopy of trees above. Faux bees and butterflies often figure in my arrangements, adding movement and a touch of whimsy to take the starch out of the scheme."

"The napkins, however, do have starch," she says. As Schultz will proudly tell you, you can take the girl out of the South, but the South remains fully in control of the girl. "These are vintage French banquet-size napkins, and each could cover half a football field. If you are wielding one of these babies and still manage to spill something on your dress, there is pretty much no hope for you. The tablecloth is a few yards of fun print from a discount fabric shop, unsewn and un-ironed. If necessity is the mother of invention, then laziness is its wacky aunt, and I love her dearly."

"Given that our guests on this night included local rose growers, wine makers, fourth-generation farmers, and an interior designer, I wanted the table to speak to our guests symbolically," she says. "High–low is my modus operandi, and I embrace the mix, believing wholeheartedly in using one's silver and pretty things even—or maybe especially—if they diverge profoundly in provenance. Because what are you saving it for? And don't say your grandchildren because what if they don't want it? (I know.)"

Schultz holds the act of breaking bread together close to her heart. "To gather friends at the table is to hold a sacred space in which we nourish our bodies and feed our souls. My hope is that we are all committed to holding this sacred space in our hearts and at home, Lord willin' and the creek don't rise."

ABOVE: Schultz loves the endless supply of olive foliage in the allée beside the house. OPPOSITE: Watermelon is always a good idea. After the party, a neighbor's pet cow enjoyed the leftover melons.

Charley

SCHULTZ DISHES ON DINNER PARTIES

• A relaxed, confident, slightly bossy hostess (or host) is key. When you are relaxed, your guests can be, too. Be completely organized and leave little for the last minute. Hire help if you can.

• Arrival is the crucial moment when guests decide, if unconsciously, whether this is going to be fun. Dim the lights and cue the votive candles. Play lively music, but softly enough to talk over. (Turn it off during dinner; life is distracting enough.) Give guests a drink the instant they walk in. Pre-poured glasses of wine prevent a rush at the bar. Offer nonalcoholic options, too. As a (slightly bossy) hostess, make introductions. Scan the group for wayward souls and wing them in.

• Have a seating plan, however small or informal your party. It saves a world of fumbling and possibly hurt feelings. Place cards are fine, but names scribbled on scrap paper will do. Seat kindred spirits together, whether they are live wires or wallflowers. They will be most comfortable and best amused with their own sort.

Rancho la Zaca

the bee cottage wine
CHARDONNAY 2015
the bee cottage wine
CHARDONNAY 2015

PREVIOUS SPREAD: Schultz is all about high–low, here using melamine plates from Pottery Barn in two patterns, vintage green stemware, heirloom silver goblets, and mercury glass votives. Centerpieces are mostly dahlias and zinnias from the garden, with roses from friends and guests Gracie and Ryan Poulson of Grace Rose Farm in Santa Ynez. Schultz rubber-stamped butterflies on the place cards. ABOVE: One of the few formal elements of the landscape is the grove of olive trees created by Los Angeles-based landscape designer Art Luna. Many decorative fabrics come in fifty-four-inch widths, making them easily adapted as tablecloths for rectangular tables, no sewing required. OPPOSITE, CLOCKWISE FROM TOP LEFT: A rendering of one of the majestic oaks that dot the property adorns personalized napkins. Watermelon-, peach-, and citrus-inspired cocktails do double duty as decorative elements on the bar. A chilled gazpacho garnished with herbs makes for a refreshing appetizer. A few pieces of inherited Mexican silver, like this commodious bowl, echo the ranch's history as an early Mexican land grant.

Front Yard Courtyard

Courtnay Tartt Elias
Houston, Texas

Sometimes the best ideas spring from a frustrating situation, as designer Courtnay Tartt Elias of Creative Tonic discovered at her home in the Tanglewood neighborhood of Houston. "The houses on my street are set way back from the curb with huge lawns, which was perfect for my three boys to play all their games when they were growing up," she says. But when Elias's next-door neighbors tore down their existing house and sited their new home closer to the street, it changed everything. "The house effectively blocks the gate that leads to our backyard and pool."

When Courtnay and husband Mark became "free birds" (her charming phrase for empty nesters) with more time to relax and entertain, they came up with a solution to the dilemma. "Instead of reworking the backyard, we decided to create a courtyard on the front of the house," says the designer. "The front yard is so big that we won't miss the twenty feet used for the courtyard." Their front yard courtyard idea was born.

As Elias explains, they struggled with the design for the space a bit. "Our 1980s stucco house is contemporary in spirit, so at first, I was thinking of a mid-century cantilevered treatment," she says. "When that did not feel right, I decided to call Michael Landrum, a favorite Houston architect. He came up with the most elegant plan." Landrum took his inspiration from the old Hollywood Regency style used in the Trousdale Estates neighborhood of Los Angeles—a masterful collection of modern homes built in the 1950s to 1970s by some of California's most sought-after architects and a favorite of celebrities. (Elvis Presley and Groucho Marx lived there.)

"Michael designed the front courtyard to be an engaging integration with the house," says Elias. "A wall connects the new terrace to the existing garage structure. It is slightly curved and is pierced with metal trellis inserts. We live on a friendly cul-de-sac, so we did not want a solid wall that would completely block out neighbors."

With the architecture settled, Elias took the reins to create her specialty—happy, colorful rooms with personality and practicality. For the built-in banquette, she was inspired by the stucco designs of the Greek islands and the haciendas of Mexico. "I chose faded blue zellige tile for the wall and white oak for the cabinetry," she says. "The white oak is repeated on the ceiling to tie everything together."

Then she added a periwinkle blue, white, and green palette with her favorite cheerful stripe, accented with a star fabric and lots of dressmaker details—pom-poms, fringe, and tape

Courtnay Tartt Elias and her husband, Mark, carefully considered how they wanted to use their home's outdoor space. Indoor accents such as blue-and-white porcelain give the covered courtyard the feeling of a true living room.

trims. "In a covered area, you can treat the outdoor space just like you would an interior room, so I like to have fun and be creative," Elias says.

For the furniture, the designer went in a fresh direction by reworking some old wood pieces. She had them stripped down and restuffed to bring them back to life. She completed the decor with blue-and-white porcelain, a wicker pagoda, mirrors, fabric poufs, and garden stools.

Outside the covered area, an artificial turf lawn is ready for bocce ball, ping-pong, cornhole, and picnics any time of year. String lights glow after dark, and a cigar-smoking area is ready for after-dinner gatherings full of lively conversation. As Elias says, "It is always a party in the courtyard. Except for the hottest months of the summer, my husband and I basically live out here. The versatility makes it ideal for a crowd."

ABOVE: Elias welcomes guests to her front courtyard entertaining space at her Houston home. BELOW: Inspired by mid-century California style, the front facade of the Elias house in Houston features impactful repetition of shapes and openings, shrubs and trees. OPPOSITE: The family loves to play games, so the turfed space includes a bocce ball court. The artificial turf lawn looks beautiful year-round with little maintenance. FOLLOWING SPREAD: In the courtyard's covered area, the designer punched up traditional French-style indoor furniture using a fabric combination of jaunty stars and stripes.

A HOME FOR ALL SEASONS DANIELLE ROLLINS
JAY JEFFERS COLLECTED COOL

ELIAS'S TIPS FOR ENTERTAINING

- Forage your yard for floral materials. Hydrangea blossoms make impactful, long-lasting floral arrangements if you cut the stems under water.
- Always offer a drink first thing. Having a special cocktail premixed kicks the festivities off with flair.
- If weather permits, take indoor chairs outside for extra seating. Bringing something fancy to the outdoors adds a note of nonchalance to the party.
- Layer your table linens and china for a lush, abundant look. Mix china patterns to add contrasting colors. Your tablecloth does not have to cover the entire table. Drape it across the middle of the table for a casual, picnic table effect.
- Do not forget lighting. Wind lots of string lights into trees and shrubbery for a magical vibe after the sun sets.

THE HOUSE OF GLAM
A HOME FOR ALL SEASONS DANIELLE ROLLINS
JAY JEFFERS COLLECTED COOL

ABOVE: Elias loves mixing colors and patterns in her table settings. OPPOSITE, CLOCKWISE FROM TOP LEFT: In Elias's front yard courtyard, a built-in stucco bench provides seating on one side, with additional chairs pulled up for alfresco meals. The two-sided fireplace opens up the covered space to the outdoors, and a spray of yellow tulips is a colorful exclamation point. On the banquette, a series of pillows in the same fabrics shows off elaborate trim applications. Courtney wanted to include husband Mark in planning the space, so they created a cigar-smoking nook.

A Memorable Feast

Barry Darr Dixon and Will Thomas
Warrenton, Virginia

As the calendar inches closer toward the end of November, Elway Hall, situated in the bucolic horse country of Warrenton, Virginia, settles into the familiar rhythms of the season. The ginkgo, maple, and oak trees that anchor its rolling hills burst into a blaze of fiery color against a clear blue sky. The goats, sheep, and chickens thicken their furry and feathery coats in preparation for much chillier temperatures just around the corner. And the cutting garden—abloom with peonies, roses, and dahlias in previous months—begins winding down for a long winter's nap.

Inside Elway, homeowners Barry Darr Dixon and Will Thomas prepare to host their Thanksgiving feast, with a guest list made up of family members, neighbors, and friends who have become like family. As a much-in-demand designer, Dixon creates richly detailed interiors that take cues from his encyclopedic memory bank of design references. Thomas, a former broadcast journalist and now a senior vice president of Sotheby's International Real Estate, handles all the meal planning and preparation with a seasoned negotiator's skill for knowing when to stick to the script and when to improvise. The duo's respective talents make an invitation to Elway a coveted one, but never more so than on a day like Thanksgiving.

"I light a lot of candles and never set the table the same way twice, whether we have a house full of guests or it's just the two of us and Dinah [their beloved wire fox terrier]," said Dixon. "Some treasured pieces travel from table to table and year to year, but I never want a repeat performance." Thomas added, "Barry usually stays out of the kitchen while I'm cooking, and I will have no idea what he's doing with the flowers and the table, which makes for a fun surprise. He loves the drama of a big reveal."

For this Thanksgiving, guests are in for a truly unexpected reveal as they'll be loading up in buggies and caravanning down the lane to have dinner in Elway's restored dairy barn. "I was inspired by the idea of the splendor of a baroque feast juxtaposed against the rusticity of the barn," said Dixon. With its aged copper roof, heart pine floors, and vaulted chestnut timbers in the loft above, the barn "almost feels like a sanctum with a wonderful spiritual quality," he continued. "It's the closest thing we have to a chapel on the property."

As Thomas sets to his kitchen assignments, cooking Dixon's favorite family recipes, Dixon and dear friend and floral designer Barbara Hamilton return to the barn to finish setting the stage for dinner. Hamilton's arrangements of roses, ilex branches, and greenery foraged from the property mingle with mottled gourds and pumpkins. As a final touch, Dixon threads a wild tangle of vines across the groaning board and chalkboard menu and gives one last check to make sure each serving piece

Barry Darr Dixon imagined a baroque feast in the early 20th-century barn and collaborated with floral designer Barbara Hamilton on arrangements of roses and ilex amid gourds and foraged vines that spill throughout the tableau.

is in its proper place for the turkey and array of side dishes to be delivered a few minutes ahead of the rest of the party.

As guests arrive, they pause to say hello to Betty and Lou, the goats who serve as the barn's unofficial greeters-in-chief, and then ascend the stairs for the big reveal. With champagne flutes in hand, they take in a setting that looks like it could be an Old Master still life painting come to real life in a Virginia barn. As everyone finds their seats at the table (Dinah's is underneath with her own dog-friendly plate of roasted turkey and sweet potatoes), Dixon and Thomas raise their glasses and make a toast to the good company, good food, and good times they gratefully share at Elway Hall.

ABOVE: Guests are always pampered with warm hospitality, delicious food, and a beautifully-designed environment, whether at the main house or in the barn. OPPOSITE, CLOCKWISE FROM TOP LEFT: Dixon and Thomas, here with their dog Dinah, invite friends year-round to their home in Warrenton, Virginia, but they particularly love hosting during the holidays. Ham biscuits are served on a transferware platter personalized with the house's name, a treasured gift from a neighbor. Thomas wrote the menu on the chalkboard behind the buffet table, which is laden with his efforts in the kitchen, including roasted acorn squash heaped in an aptware bowl. FOLLOWING SPREAD: Dixon said, "I light a lot of candles and never set the table the same way twice. Some treasured pieces travel from table to table and year to year, but I never want a repeat a performance."

DIXON'S HINTS FOR AUTUMNAL DECOR

- We forage the farm for decorations for the Thanksgiving table. I cut branches from the maple trees, the ginkgos, and the oaks, with their leaves all offering different hues.
- We grow gourds of all sorts and put them everywhere, on the dining table, piled up in the entry to the barn, tucked under tables in buckets.
- Branches of berries add another texture to floral arrangements and help out as tall, vertical elements on tables.
- I like to use bowls of like fruit on the tables, like persimmons. It adds a baroque touch that's perfect for a feast.
- I have a pair of tall candelabra that I fill with candles. They cast the most magical glow over the Thanksgiving table.

BELOW: The warm palette of reds, oranges, and umbers—colors that Dixon gravitates toward in both his decorating and his product design—echoes the late-autumn landscape. OPPOSITE, CLOCKWISE FROM TOP LEFT: Desserts await on a nearby table, anchored with a massive grapevine from Napa Valley, a nod to Thomas's California roots. Dixon commissioned the tea service from a silversmith during a trip to Argentina. Dixon designed the henhouse, which echoes architectural elements of the main house. Homegrown pumpkins decorate almost every nook and cranny. The table is set for dinner with a mix of family heirlooms, antiques collected during European travels, and new pieces found in local shops.

Rooftop Reverie

Fiona Tilley and Gurhan
New York, NY

Years ago, if you had told a young Fiona Tilley that in 2019 she would be a former Wall Street banker married to a Turkish jeweler and running the company that sells his designs, she might not have believed you. What she would have believed is that she would be the caretaker of a fabulous garden. For all her years as a world-traveling, hard-charging investment banker, gardening is a love that has never left her. "My mother is an avid gardener, and my father studied horticulture," she says. In fact, her last name is derived from "tiller of the soil," the result of an ancestor who migrated from England to Australia and established one of the country's first public gardens there.

"Although I am Australian, I have lived in the States for thirty-three years, so this is definitely home for me," says Tilley, who moved to New York with the company J. P. Morgan after practicing law. Her husband, jewelry designer Gurhan, came to America ten years later, and their courtship was as serendipitous as any romantic comedy.

"I met Gurhan in 1995, when I was still a banker," says Tilley. "I was on vacation with a girlfriend in a small coastal town in Turkey. Truthfully, I fell in love with Turkey before I fell in love with the jewelry before I fell in love with the jeweler," she says, laughing. She spent the entire day in Gurhan's store. "Something about his pieces really spoke to me," she says. She asked the clerk if she could meet the designer. "Can I look him up?" she remembers asking. "No," was the answer. "'He is a cranky old man, and he does not speak English,' the clerk said to me," remembers Tilley. But the pleasantly persistent redhead did not give up.

"A couple of weeks later my friend and I were in Istanbul, and I called on this supposed cranky old man. I remember two things. First of all, he spoke beautiful English. Second of all, he was not cranky. He was wonderfully welcoming and invited us to his home."

For Tilley it was love at first sight, "even though I did not believe in love at first sight," she says. The pair stayed in touch by telephone for sixteen months until Gurhan moved to New York. They were engaged soon after and married in 1999, the year Tilley left banking to run business operations for Gurhan.

In the wake of 9/11, when the couple set about looking for a new apartment, it had to meet three criteria: It had to be downtown (in a show of solidarity with the wounded part of their city), it had to have a view, and it had to have a garden. The West Village apartment they found had it all: a wonderful downtown feel, 360-degree views of the city, and an 1,800-square-foot roof perfect for a garden.

To make the most of her rooftop space, Fiona Tilley created separate areas for dining and lounging.

Though the couple both love the garden, it is unquestionably Tilley's domain. "I do all the work up there," she says proudly. "I love to get my hands dirty." The result of her work is an eclectic, bohemian, magical space so lush it is hard to remember that everything is in containers. She loves trees and has an array of willows, column oaks, birches, mulberries, poplars, and maples. A trellis laden with wisteria, along with clusters of annuals and perennials, attracts the locals. "The birds love the trees, and the butterflies love the flowers," says Tilley.

She appreciates the order and restraint of other gardens but is not drawn to that style. "I love the craziness of the English garden. I love mixing the colors," she says. "I am constantly trying new things and changing it up. Gurhan is always saying to me, 'You do not have to redecorate the roof!'" she says. But for a woman whose life has been so rewarded by being open to possibility, how can she resist?

ABOVE: Lounge chairs face west, perfect for watching the sun set over the Hudson River. Objects from the couple's frequent trips around the world fill the garden. OPPOSITE, CLOCKWISE FROM TOP LEFT: Tilley takes a free-spirited approach to entertaining, offering an array of bubbly beverages to guests lucky enough to be invited to her rooftop garden. The garden is filled with objects such as this one that the couple collect on their trips around the world. Petunias climb over a window frame used as a trellis. FOLLOWING SPREAD: Behind the beautiful table, a row of trees creates a screen and masks the wall.

ABOVE: Tilley used the rooftop heating vents as a backdrop for a trio of planted pots. OPPOSITE, FROM LEFT: A trellis of wisteria invites birds to stay awhile. Tomatoes flourish in coir-lined baskets along a ledge.

TILLEY'S TIPS FOR POTTING PLANTS

- Choose the best potting soil you can afford. Use a high-quality bagged mix designed specifically for containers; it will have perlite compost and other materials to keep the mix loose and aerated.
- Ensure good drainage: Lack of drainage is a top reason container plantings fail. Some pots do not have drainage holes and you will need to drill them before using them as a planter. Excess water that stays in the root zone means plant roots cannot breathe—they need oxygen, too. Soggy soil also creates anaerobic conditions, which foster harmful bacteria and kill off the helpful bacteria.
- Skip the rocks: A popular notion persists that you should add rocks or broken pieces of pottery to the bottoms of your containers. While it seems logical, studies have proved that in most cases, this does not work and may even slow down drainage.
- Pot plants with similar needs: If you plan a multispecies pot, ensure that the plants you select thrive in the same conditions. Most commonly, that means planting sun-loving together and not mixing them in the same container with shade-loving plants.
- Pick the right size pot: Five-gallon pots work for tomatoes, peppers, ornamental shrubs, and container gardens with multiple types of plants. Two- to three-gallon pots serve for herbs and many flowers like begonias, salvia, and short ornamental grasses. Use one-gallon pots for marigolds and other small annual flowers, lettuce, and accent plantings of a single small plant.

Big Easy Breezy

Jane Scott Hodges
New Orleans, Louisiana

Jane Scott Hodges may reign supreme over embroidered linens with her Leontine Linens line, but when she entertains, she is just like any other hostess, a little worried by the scope of effort required to pull it off. Such was the scene on the day of a dinner party she hosted at her New Orleans home. The occasion was a visit by a group of friends from Charlotte, North Carolina. All members of the Mint Museum's travel club, the Crown Society, the guest list included several of Hodges's dear friends. The stakes were raised beyond the usual affair, and Hodges was preparing to host a seated dinner for thirty-two on her terrace.

"This group is so special. We really wanted to put on the dog for them," says Hodges. "We hired a jazz trio to play, and we opened the windows to the terrace, so it and the dining room were like one big room. We covered three tables in Indian block-print tablecloths borrowed from a pal," says Hodges. "But they are bedspread size so my husband had to run out and get Saints gold clothes for underneath." Then, she set about composing place settings by calling on the resources of neighbors. Three different but complementary china patterns appeared on each table. "We have a lot of friends on the street, and we all share china. We scratch each other's back for these occasions."

An Indian theme grew out of the block-print fabric, with the oranges and pinks of Indian textiles reflected in the centerpieces of marigolds and purple scabiosa by floral designer Pamela Dennis. "I am not great at flowers," Hodges admits, "so I begged her to do them." Place settings, however, are her forte. "It's always fun for me to dress the tables," she says. "We mixed china patterns with orange, rust, and rosy tones. I like using natural woven chargers under the plates to distinguish them visually. The layers of color make the tables feel warmer. It is not about perfection."

To continue the Indian theme, Hodges enlisted the talents behind Saffron, a great New Orleans restaurant. "I love their food and knew it would be a hit for this group," she says. The menu included curried gumbo, roasted oysters, tandoori squash, and chicken biryani for melding the flavors of New Orleans and India. Hand-painted menu cards with a marigold motif lent a touch of art to the tables. A macaron cake crowned the feast with its extravagant flourish.

Though Hodges is a master entertainer, she admits that throwing a dinner party does have its stressors. "I do love entertaining at home," she says. "It is hard work, but people are so appreciative of your efforts. It allows you to create an experience for your friends and also get to share it with them. It is the nicest gift you can offer."

Jane Scott Hodges takes a moment to catch her breath before her guests arrive. "I found a dress that matched my scheme," she says of her ivory and aubergine frock.

ABOVE, CLOCKWISE FROM TOP LEFT: Mojitos were served in julep glasses—a classic mash-up of Cuban and Southern influences. Customized place cards let the guests know their presence was much appreciated. A macaron cake is a specialty of New Orleans bakers—this one customized with the party's palette. A hand-painted menu card maps out the evening's menu by the chefs at Saffron restaurant. OPPOSITE: Marigolds, tulips, and scabiosa reflect the orange and purples of the table linens. "I got the woven baskets from Alex Papachristidis in New York," says Hodges.

Philip

BELOW: A glass by New Orleans glassblower Ridge Walker mingles with French porcelain and a woven place mat. Hodges's embroidered table linens are the jewel in the crown in every table she sets. OPPOSITE: A crowd of patrons of the Mint Museum in Charlotte, North Carolina, descended on the Big Easy for a weekend of museum visits and revelry. The hostess welcomed the group to her home for a charming and chic seated dinner. The group lapped up the New Orleans hospitality on her terrace.

HOW **HODGES** CREATES A GORGEOUS TABLE OUTSIDE

- First, start off with its foundation—the tablecloth. I find hand-blocked fabric to be the easiest to build off.
- The next key ingredient is a woven place mat. It gives texture when placed between the tablecloth and your china. Create a color story based on your china pattern with place mats and napkins in the same color family.
- When creating a tablescape, I gravitate toward branches and other organic materials like woven wood baskets, pheasant feathers, and, of course, seasonal fruit. These fill up the table space whether placed directly in the center or strewn around plates.
- I love handblown glass and currently love the work of glassblower Ridge Walker. I mix up different silhouettes to add interest.
- I collect tiny stone bowls and scatter them around the table with snacks like nuts, chocolate, or cheese straws in them.

Luncheon on the Loggia

Mish Tworkowski
Palm Beach, Florida

The studio where jewelry designer Mish Tworkowski creates and sells his coveted designs is located on Phipps Plaza in Palm Beach, where bougainvillea tumbles in profusion from the walls and the Addison Mizner–designed building evokes the glamorous history of the tony enclave. It is, quite literally, a jewel box. And it is also where Tworkowski and his husband, architect and business partner Joseph Singer, like to entertain.

The pair enlisted designer Katie Ritter to concoct the colorful, spirited interiors that exude a sense of fun. Most enchanting is the "nook" as Tworkowski calls it, a trellised space painted lavender, or as Tworkwoski puts it, "Mish purple." With orchids mounted on the trellis, the entire spectrum of Palm Beach color is represented, from orchid pink to lemon yellow to Lilly Pulitzer orange. "For me who loves color, Palm Beach is the perfect place to be," says Tworkowski. "We love the warm weather, and I love being able to dress in bright colors." Having been named to the International Best Dressed List, he takes as much care with his wardrobe as he does with his work for Mish Fine Jewelry.

His designs are a celebration of horticulture, gemstones, and color. Flowers are a constant motif, with chrysanthemums, hibiscus, anemones, poppies, pansies, camelias, orchids, and gardenias, among others, making their appearance in his collection. His statement earrings often feature interesting materials like peridot, fossilized coral, and petrified wood.

Recently, Tworkowski and Singer gathered friends for a luncheon on the loggia, which serves as the de facto entrance to the shop. For the table, Tworkowski unleashed a floraganza with botanical prints in all the colors he loves. "We used a Matouk citrus print for the tablecloth," he says. "The chair seats are all covered in different Svenskt Tenn prints." Even the china featured a bamboo leaf pattern. "We collect restaurant ware, primarily from auctions," he says. "This was a bamboo pattern from the 1940s, which works with our bamboo flatware." The stemware is another collectible by Biot. It features bubbles in the glass, which was at one time considered undesirable in glassmaking. But Biot took pride in flouting "old" ideas and proudly manufactured bubble glass for a new, more adventurous consumer.

Floral centerpieces by Susan Lewis echoed the riotous colors of the textiles, with hibiscus, protea, and birds-of-paradise. The copious bougainvillea spilled down the table, giving the table a lush, layered look. Tworkowski is fastidious about place cards and takes great pains to think through the guest list to pick the perfect table partners. "Everyone wants to feel great when seated," he says. "We have started quite a few friendships." As anyone who has had the pleasure of meeting Tworkowski already knows, he is someone who immediately becomes your friend. And is that not the point of every gathering around a table?

A maximalist Palm Beach style reigns on the lunch table with botanical prints like the Matouk tablecloth and chair fabrics by Swedish firm Svenskt Tenn. The ever-modern Svenskt Tenn prints from the 1940s add a layer of floral influence to the table.

ABOVE: Birds-of-paradise, hibiscus, and protea form classic tropical centerpieces for the festive table, which is flanked by potted garcinias and hibiscus. OPPOSITE, CLOCKWISE FROM TOP LEFT: Joseph Singer, left, and Mish Tworkowski in the lattice room designed by Katie Ridder. The duo's Irish setter–golden retriever mix, Bobo, greets the guests on the loggia. Legendary Palm Beach architect Addison Mizner designed the building that houses Mish Fine Jewelry. FOLLOWING SPREAD: Tworkowski and Singer shop for tableware from the 1940s at auction and used for this party bamboo-themed flatware to set a tropical table. Venetian glass goblets, also from the 1940s, add their own mid-century magic.

Mish
Menu
starter
main
with salad of
gem lettuce
dessert

TWORKOWSKI'S TIPS FOR ENTERTAINING OUTDOORS

- Serve excellent wine and offer both a white and red regardless of what you are serving. A large silver container filled with ice keeps the white chilled to perfection in Palm Beach's balmy clime.
- Do place cards. It makes for better conversation and happier guests. I made pressed flower plastic cards for this party to allow for the humidity.
- Make a delightful, engaging toast in between one of the courses. Bonus points for acknowledging any guest's significant milestone.
- Use large starched and super-pressed napkins. It feels special to use them outdoors.
- If time allows, make a dessert. It's a special way to cap the meal—and who doesn't love a little something sweet?

BELOW: Place cards put convivial personalities together for maximum fun. OPPOSITE, CLOCKWISE FROM TOP LEFT: A nineteenth-century Majolica vase continues the tropical theme on the dining table. A dessert of mango pie conforms to the established palette of the party. Tworkowski and Singer cultivate orchids at home and rotate them into the shop as they bloom. Tworkowski and Singer collect silver spoons engraved with the names of Florida cities.

A Farm Fresh Fête

Mary Celeste Beall
Walland, Tennessee

Nestled deep in the Smoky Mountains, Blackberry Farm is more than just a luxurious resort. It is an emblem of the beauty and serenity that East Tennessee offers, a place where guests can escape the rush of modern life and immerse themselves in nature, good food, and the richness of Southern hospitality. But what makes this farm special is not just the lush landscape or the gourmet meals—it is the vision of a remarkable family, the Bealls.

In 1975, when Chris and Sandy Beall bought a charming inn in Walland, Tennessee, for their family, they could not have known that their discovery would eventually evolve into one of the most acclaimed luxury properties in the country. Blackberry Farm was born out of a love for the land, for a life of simplicity, and for the idea that luxury is not about opulence, but about intimacy with a place and with people.

The resort now includes Blackberry Mountain, a wellness spa, and is helmed by Mary Celeste Beall, Chris and Sandy's daughter-in-law, who took the reins when her husband, Sam, died in a tragic accident in 2016. The transition had its challenges. "I had to prove myself because I was Sam's wife and I lived in this beautiful house at the farm and I had a housekeeper and I had all these people helping me. And I felt like I had to show them that I was capable. One of the hardest things for me was finally saying, 'You know what? You do not have to know everything about every department.' It is not realistic to spread yourself that thin. And what you should do is focus on what your strengths are, and trust people and you have got to delegate."

Now with over a decade under her belt, Beall is hitting her stride and has embraced the Blackberry Farm aesthetic. On a recent weekend night, she gathered a group of women friends and her daughter Cameron for an alfresco dinner. "When the garden is in full bloom, you just have to pause and enjoy with good friends," she says. "So I invited friends from Knoxville and Blackberry Farm to join me for dinner. Gathering around the table is truly my favorite thing, especially in the garden on a beautiful summer evening. I kept it intimate so we could all connect at one table."

The table decor and food all reflected the bounty of East Tennessee. "When you have the summer garden to work with, you just lean all in—simple, fresh, and colorful. At the peak of the season, there's no reason to hold back. Zinnias are the queens of giving more and more with each good snip, so we created full, vibrant arrangements that brought the beauty of the garden right to the table," she says.

For the drinks table, the team fashioned loose arrangements of zinnias, hydrangeas, and cosmos in locally-made pottery. "The mix of refined tableware with rustic elements creates a balance between elegance and approachability," says Mary Celeste Beall.

The food, like the flowers, linked the dinner to the land, with farm-grown tri-star and sugar snap beans, pan-fried squash blossoms, and house madeleines with trout roe and crème fraîche. "I wanted to keep it casual, so we had a lot of small tastes, which was fun and relaxing," she says. "Having a variety of bites helps cover different dietary restrictions, which is always a bonus. I love adding flowers to the plate, not only for their beauty, but because I try to 'eat the rainbow,' and feel like these gorgeous petals are packing some special nutrition." As the dinner wound down, and dusk approached, the guests all agreed that Girls Garden Party should become an annual event—a moment to celebrate summer and each other.

ABOVE: Beall dressed up a classic picnic table with soft plaid table linens and refined tableware. “Indoor” tableware used outdoors is always a signifier of good times to be had. OPPOSITE, CLOCKWISE FROM TOP LEFT: Beall has a special place in her heart for zinnias. “They continue to be a rewarding favorite of mine with such happy energy.” An outdoor covered pavilion, called Yallarhammer, is used for large gatherings and special events hosted at the farm. FOLLOWING SPREAD LEFT: Beall’s youngest daughter helps with the weeding. FOLLOWING SPREAD RIGHT: Beall set the places with a white pottery charger, a blue dinner plate, and a white dessert plate with delicate hand detailing. Glass vases for the dinner table arrangements amplify the vivid colors of the summer blooms. Fried squash blossoms and stuffed snapdragon blooms bring the farm to the table.

BEALL'S FARM TABLE INGREDIENTS

"Whenever we sit in the garden, we want it to be open and inviting," says Beall. Here, she breaks down the ingredients of the floral arrangements and the festive table.

FLOWERS

- Celosia (Cockscomb or Plume Celosia): The bright orange and red feathery plumes or brainlike textures add height and a unique shape to the bouquet.
- Cosmos: Light and airy, these pink and magenta blooms bring a whimsical, wildflower feel.
- Hydrangeas: The clusters of greenish blooms provide fullness and contrast against the small, more delicate flowers.
- Lisianthus: The soft pink blooms offer a delicate, ruffled texture similar to roses.
- Veronica (Speedwell): The tall, slender, purple spikes give elegance and movement.
- Zinnias: Growing up, zinnias meant summer. My mom always had them growing in our yard with vases of them all over our house. Bright and bold, these flowers come in shades of orange, pink, and yellow, adding a cheerful, rustic touch.
- Garden greenery and filler flowers: Various leafy greens and tiny blossoms provide texture and depth, complementing the larger focal flowers.

COLOR PALETTE AND ELEMENTS

- Soft blues and whites: The layered dinnerware features a combination of a large white pottery charger, a blue dinner plate, and a small white plate with delicate hand detailing.
- Warm wood tones: The natural wood table provides an organic, rustic contrast to the refined dishware.
- Plaid textiles: The light plaid runner and napkin, in soft blues and whites, contribute to a relaxed, garden-inspired charm.
- Floral accents: Fresh zinnias, wildflowers, and seasonal blooms in shades of pink, orange, and deep purple are arranged in glass vases of varying heights and colors (amber, pink, and clear glass).
- Gold and amber hues: The gold-leaf, patterned tumbler brings warmth and texture to the table as it sits beside the brighter-colored vases, adding a subtle hint that is delicate alongside the classic, simple wineglasses.

Mary Celeste

ABOVE, CLOCKWISE FROM TOP LEFT: Beet hummus with horseradish and sumac made a garden-fresh appetizer. A farm cat, Hyssop, is a beloved fixture on the property. "You will often find her napping in the garden shed," says Beall. A Garden Shed daiquiri made with Don Q rum, Poli Miele honey liqueur, lemon, and garden herbs garnished with Johnny Jump Up flower petals was the party's signature cocktail. Light main courses of an heirloom tomato salad and grilled okra rounded out the menu. Handwritten place cards and menu cards penned by gardener John Coykendall and a single zinnia add a personal, thoughtful detail. OPPOSITE: Beall raises a glass to her friends and to the farm's summer bounty. Breezy dresses were the official party attire.

Pool House Panache

Heather Chadduck
Birmingham, Alabama

In a historic neighborhood in Birmingham, Alabama, designer Heather Chadduck has carved out an elegant retreat steps from her Georgian clapboard house where traditional rooms serve as a backdrop for a display of fresh, timeless grace notes. The site of the new pool and pool house required heavy machinery and plenty of patience as it was carved out of the hillside. Now, with the pool house finished and furnished, it is frequently the site of gathering with friends and celebrations small and large.

Chadduck, with her eternally calm demeanor, approaches entertaining like she decorates a room, laying on tableware she has collected over the years, souvenirs from her travels, and linens from the region's best sources for an effect that is sumptuous but not stuffy. As with all she touches, traditional flourishes mingle with flea market finds in a stylish mix of English, French, Asian, and Southern style. Breezy striped side chairs contrast with the more formal double dolphin-based consoles. Normally outfitted in outdoor lounge furniture, the pool house gets plentiful use in the summer, when Chadduck and husband David Hillegas take a dip and convene in the pool house to reflect on their respective days.

For summer entertaining, they remove the loungers and replace them with a folding table and chinoiserie chairs borrowed from the dining room. "I love bringing fancy chairs outdoors," says Chadduck. The chairs are covered in a ticking stripe applied horizontally that brings the formality down a notch. A voluminous table skirt of Rose Cumming chintz provides a base layer for Chadduck's concoction of color and texture. "Chintz makes it like a ballgown," she says. The fabric is coated in a glaze and then ironed to achieve its stiff and slightly shiny texture.

Upon that base, Chadduck layered brass and rattan chargers, pewter and brass cups, white cabbage-leaf china, bamboo flatware, and Leontine Linens napkins in a buoyant concoction. In the center of the table, a lavish arrangement of pale peach roses, geranium leaves, white peonies, mountain laurel berries, and satsuma branches offer a dose of sunset color and summer fragrance. Many of the plant materials were grown in Chadduck's new greenhouse, including the citrus.

Before starting her own design business, Chadduck inspired millions

"I grew up having dinner on white cabbage plates because my mother, Suga, loved them. They are versatile enough for all seasons," says Heather Chadduck. She likes to mix different metals on her table, including a brass tray and pewter and brass lassi cups she brought back from a trip to India.

of readers through her editorial work at *Cottage Living*, *Coastal Living*, and *Southern Living*. She later took on the role of designer in residence to Colonial Williamsburg, where she designed and lived in a historic house in the town along with David and their dog, Louise. Chadduck began her career in the 1990s creating dreamy retreats—literally—for the catalogues of bedding manufacturers, including Peacock Alley, Yves Delorme, and Neiman Marcus. Her pool house now offers its own magical, transportive allure.

ABOVE: Chadduck laid the floor tiles straight rather than on the diagonal to pay homage to Round Hill in Jamaica, where she and David were married. OPPOSITE, CLOCKWISE FROM TOP LEFT: Chadduck poses beside one of many "peeling, crumbly" large containers she collects and uses to great effect. A crusty French iron urn adds patina to the table. Chadduck grew many of the elements in her centerpiece in her new greenhouse, including Meyer lemons, satsumas, kumquats, and scented geranium. A potted philodendron, green Moroccan pottery, and shells make a pretty, simple vignette. FOLLOWING SPREAD: Shell motif sconces flank the high window in the pool house. Chadduck found the double dolphin table base in an antiques market and topped it with soapstone. An antique bracket shell sconce was fashioned from found objects. The tablecloth is made of Rose Cumming chintz. The white cabbage ware is from Clemontín, and the napkins are from Leontine Linens.

CHADDUCK'S FAVORITE THINGS FOR A GARDEN SETTING

- Moroccan metals: I love hand-forged brass and pewter vessels. They are great for styling flowers and take on a great patina over time. And they do not shatter if you drop one.
- Foraged greenery: If you have an orange safety vest, it's a license to forage along the highway, or you can source from your own yard.
- Pineapple motifs: It is the most classic emblem of Southern hospitality. My house is named the Pineapple House because of the existing pineapple door knocker that was on the house when we moved in.
- Orange: Pops of orange, such as satsumas and kumquats, always give energy to a room or a table. It is a delicious color.

Heather

GARDENS

Joie de Vivre

Sharon Santoni
Normandy, France

Sharon Santoni is a woman of immense patience. When she and her husband, Eric, first laid eyes on the two-hundred-year-old farmhouse in Normandy that would become their home, they had two toddlers. By the time they moved in, Santoni was about to give birth to their fourth child. And then the business of raising children delayed her full focus on the gardens. But eventually the seasons of life rolled around, and she was able to turn her attention to the trees, beds, and vines on the property.

Santoni greets each day with a stroll through her gardens. "Before the phone starts ringing in the morning, I slip out the terrace door barefoot, cup of tea in hand, dogs at my feet," she says. "The doves are cooing, the cuckoos are shrilling, and I am carrying my secateurs to cut flowers from the garden and then head down to the potager to harvest zucchini."

Even during the intensive child-rearing years, Santoni was preparing the garden for the splendor it now exudes. Whenever she had a few minutes to herself, she would pull the snowdrops and narcissus from the parterres they had overrun and relocate them under the magnolias. She also planted the climbing roses early on, giving them a head start to climb the walls of the farmhouse and outbuildings. By the time her children were grown, she had a clear vision for the quartet of parterres filled with flowers inspired by the gardens of Sissinghurst Castle, which she frequented during her childhood in Britain. "The garden is an extension of my home and it is forever changing," she says. "I love walking among the beds and editing. It is where I can be most creative."

A loose blend of nepeta, alliums, foxglove, irises, columbines, and poppies fills the parterres. A potager filled with vegetables, which is less pretty but practical, lies behind a hedge and provides homegrown ingredients for the feasts Sharon and Eric routinely host. Rhubarb from the garden frequently appears for dessert, in a delightful crumble. The garden also provides the centerpieces for Santoni's table, set in the garden where the mild climate assures an absence of insects and other pests. "I never buy cut flowers from March through October," she says. She favors a display of liqueur glasses each holding a bloom or two. "They look so pretty dotted around the table, and I like to echo colors," she says.

Not content to rest on her laurels, Santoni began writing about her garden, first in a blog, then in two books, *My Stylish French Girlfriends* and *My French Country Home*. In 2019, Santoni started a magazine, *My French Country Home: The Magazine*. She also leads tours of her favorite French resources, sharing the charm and spirit of the French countryside with an ever-widening audience. "We see beautiful things, take classes, and drink a lot of champagne," she says. "Everyone smiles all the time." Santoni appears to be in the business of joie de vivre.

The leitmotif for Sharon Santoni's gardens is climbing roses, which envelop the barn in color throughout the spring. Pale yellow 'Polka' opens tawny orange and blanches as it ages. A climbing 'Gertrude Jekyll' David Austin rose entwines a nesting box.

ABOVE: Thanks to the parterres, the property feels much larger than its modest one acre. Each parterre is a merry mixture of poppies, foxglove, sage, and catmint edged with Ilex crenata and accented by roses. BELOW: To give the terrace dining table a sense of enclosure, Santoni tucked it into a grove of potted herbs and container-grown delphinium. Comfortable wicker chairs are fitted with linen cushions whisked indoors at the mere hint of rain. OPPOSITE: Santoni holds an armload of newly-harvested stems destined for rhubarb crumble. FOLLOWING SPREAD: A classic French house and garden tableau on Santoni's property.

BELOW: Potted artemisia and euphorbia are clustered beside a teak Lutyens bench and wicker chairs. OPPOSITE, CLOCKWISE FROM TOP LEFT: A glass marquise over the door leading to the dining terrace is a typical French touch. Equally classic are the climbing vintage roses clambering up the walls above potted olive trees. Climbing hydrangeas envelop the woodshed behind a vintage metal wheelbarrow with convenient removable sides. A rain bucket catches water from the roof of the old stone barn. The 'Constance Spry' roses flourish in the ideal climate of Normandy. FOLLOWING SPREAD: Roses climb the stone facade of the barn, built in 1832.

SANTONI'S FAVORITE FLOWERS TO PLANT

- Sometimes, I bring in a fairly large quantity of something we already had. A few years ago, I planted three hundred irises.
- Last year, my husband talked me into planting gladioli, which I never thought I would do, but I was pleasantly surprised by how much I liked them.
- Every year, we put down hundreds of dahlias.
- I always order too many seeds, but at least they are easy to plant. I always do cosmos from seed. Last year, the zinnias did really well.

A Garden for Strolling

Bettie Bearden Pardee
Newport, Rhode Island

Bettie Bearden Pardee and her husband, Jonathan, were firm about one thing in their marriage. "We agreed we would never, ever build a house together," she says. But a gorgeous lot near Rosecliff mansion in his hometown of Newport, Rhode Island, became available and their position softened. They set about building a French-inspired house among the beeches, oaks, and linden trees of the property, which they named Parterre. And, fortuitously, the pair enjoyed the building process. "We have never had so much fun," she says. "We loved the chance to customize the details of our house."

Pardee is immensely influenced by historic stately homes and gardens. As an author, blogger, lecturer, and garden expert, she shares her inspirations in writing about houses and gardens she has visited. On her blog, she provides gardening tips and tricks to her followers who hang on her every account of the deer who ate all her roses the night before a garden tour, or the bunnies who rampaged in the cutting garden.

As Pardee began planning her gardens, she kept a file of tear sheets and notes for the look she was after. When she hired landscape designer Virginia Purviance to spearhead the job, she presented her with the research. "As we began discussing Bettie's garden, she handed me a scrapbook overflowing with pictures and handwritten notes," Purviance says. "Right away, I knew this was no ordinary endeavor." The first space they created is now called the winter garden, since its evergreen shrubs lend themselves to a snowy landscape in the winter. Entered through ornate iron gates, the garden is enclosed and centers on a reflecting pool.

Purviance collaborated with landscape designer Julie Toland to design a series of outdoor rooms, each with a distinct attitude. "I like to think of Parterre as a collection of smaller gardens created in the French tradition, with an American accent and a Newport sensibility," Pardee says.

"My husband's decision to surprise me with a Christmas gift of a greenhouse was a significant addition. It has a copper roof surmounted by glass panels you can open in the summer. It serves as a storage space during the winter, but in the summer it is a glorious place to host dinner parties." The Orangerie, as it is called, is the jewel in the crown of the garden, but in the winter garden a little hobbit house of a garden shed adds its own charm.

An armillary sphere adds a focal point to the parterre garden.

When Pardee entertains, the floral decorations are top of mind. "Every plant at Parterre must pass the litmus test of 'Will it enhance a flower arrangement?'" she says. A cutting garden supplies Pardee with materials for centerpieces and flower show entries. In addition to dahlias, roses, and clematis, vegetables like squash and zucchini grow in lush abandon, in sharp contrast to the tidy shapes of the formal gardens. Purviance sums it up best: "Parterre is a garden that is meant for walking around and strolling. It is not really intended for sitting. In that way, the whole layout and sequence of both house and grounds are very French."

ABOVE: Bettie Bearden Pardee designed and now sells the exuberant Parterre Bench. Situated between the Orangerie and the back lawn, the courtyard features four parterres containing 'Hally Jolivette' cherry trees. OPPOSITE: The cutting garden, along with its ferns and flowering tree species, provides material for Pardee's flower arrangements. FOLLOWING SPREAD: The winter garden, with its pigeonnier and reflecting pool, features Pardee's bench tucked into a niche in the hedge, and spring green Caisse de Versailles planters.

BELOW: A crusty cast-iron container holds a piri-piri bur. OPPOSITE: Daffodils point the way to the winter garden, accessed through a pair of imposing iron gates. FOLLOWING SPREAD: 'Eden' climbing roses adorn the Orangerie, a greenhouse that serves as storage in the winter and hosts dinner parties in the summer months.

PARDEE'S TIPS FOR DESIGNING YOUR DREAM GARDEN

- Look to the experts. Many nurseries have consulting and design services and online catalogues that illustrate garden groupings and offer plants for sale.
- Manage your expectations. Ask other garden owners and tradespeople for thoughts about budget.
- Do not forget about maintenance in time, money, and availability of services.
- Consider the relevance of a garden's entire design—style, hard or soft features, furniture, ornaments, and containers, as well as plantings.
- The "bones" of a garden (form, shape, scale) are more important than color (flowers are fleeting).
- Everything does not have to be done at one time. There is merit in installing a garden in stages (and it's easier on the budget).
- Be brave. Take that initial step (noted interior designer Bunny Williams's first garden was ordered out of a catalogue).
- Add a bench or two. If you do not have a place to sit, you will not go into the garden.

Grey Gardens

Liz Lange
East Hampton, New York

When Liz Lange rented the house known as Grey Gardens for the summer, she fell hard for it. "It was love at first sight!" she says. "I knew I wanted to get my hands on it but did not think it would ever be possible. I had the idea to offer to rent it for the next ten years—the closest thing to buying it." The house was owned at that point by *Washington Post* editor Sally Quinn, whose husband, Ben Bradlee, had recently passed away. To Lange's surprise, Quinn agreed to sell. "Her heart just wasn't in it," Lange says. So began a major renovation, restoration, and expansion of the storied property, with Lange calling on a team of architects, designers, and landscape architects to realize her vision for the house.

Originally built for Mr. and Mrs. Fleming Stanhope Phillips in the early twentieth century, it was then bought by Robert Hill and his wife, Anna Gilman Hill, a gifted garden writer and plants person. She and landscape architect Ruth Dean designed the gardens using a palette of pastels, including lavender, phlox, delphinium, and climbing rose.

The home was later bought by Phelan and Edith Beale but eventually fell into disrepair when the Beales divorced. Edith, known by many as "Big Edie," was left with no resources for the upkeep of the house. She and her daughter, "Little Edie," lived in unimaginable squalor for many years until the neglected property was acquired by Quinn and Bradlee. The couple kept all the original furniture, including heirloom wicker pieces found in the attic, and completely restored and decorated the house for their own weekend and holiday enjoyment.

The house could not have landed in better hands. The creator of Liz Lange Maternity and more recently, Figue, has a keen eye for fashion evolution. "I design for myself," she says. "In the 1990s and early 2000s, there was a cleaner, somewhat urban aesthetic that fit my life. Now, I am in a more resort-y phase. I laughingly said that I have entered my caftan years."

To honor the home's past, Lange incorporated a few nods to elegance in reference to the Beales. She has always loved the sophisticated look of film producer Bob Evans's round swimming pool in Beverly Hills, so she added one. Interior designer Mark Sikes then designed blue-and-white striped chaise longues to go along with it. Sikes also envisioned jaunty stripes in the pool pavilion, and engaged legendary decorative painter Bob Christian to paint the same stripes on the walls and ceiling for a tentlike effect.

New York-based landscape architect Deborah Nevins worked

Welcoming beds of hydrangeas blanket the approach to Grey Gardens.

with Lange to restore the Hills's pergola, walled garden, and thatched hut that had all grown a bit tired over the years. "Debby [Nevins] knew of a company in India that could fabricate the white marble planters, fountain, and furniture, so we commissioned them." The pieces are dramatic and unexpected for East Hampton, yet they work and even seem to reflect Lange's recent foray into fashions with a more international profile.

Another voice Lange incorporates into her design scheme is that of the Bridgehampton florist Michael Grim. Having known Lange for years, Grim understands and interprets her floral preferences beautifully. "Liz loves garden flowers and is never afraid of color," he says. This unfussy attitude is representative of Lange's overall ethos. "I do not take myself—or my homes—too seriously," she says. "I am mostly barefoot, but that is because I am feral. People walk in and say, 'Oh, my, should I take off my shoes?' And I always respond, 'Only if you want to.'" One might imagine the Edies somewhere nodding in approval.

ABOVE, TOP: Landscape architect Deborah Nevins located a source in India to fabricate the white marble furniture, fountain, and planters. ABOVE: Shades of blue, climbing vines, and potted plants create a jubilant welcome to Grey Gardens. OPPOSITE: Liz Lange relaxes in the pool pavilion in a caftan from her Figue fashion brand. FOLLOWING TWO SPREADS: Munder-Skiles chaise longues, designed by Mark Sikes, accompany the round pool for a charming outdoor tableau. The pavilion beyond was drawn by architects Bories & Shearron. The marble fountain centers a geometric square garden of alternating boxwoods and topiary trees, poised as if to dance together.

LANGE'S
ENTERTAINING TIPS

- The best number of guests at a party is around eight people. That way, you can have one conversation, which the whole table can participate in—rather than lots of little sidebar chats.
- Instead of asking everyone what their eating preferences and restrictions are (so unglamorous), I just serve a wide variety of food so that there is something for everyone.
- I always set my outdoor table with a mix of my best china, stemware, and linens interspersed with fun vintage finds. If you save all your good tableware for special occasions, you will rarely get to use and enjoy it.
- When I got married, Eddie Munves, the late owner of James Robinson in New York City, told me that I should use my sterling flatware every day and just throw it in the dishwasher. It was great advice that I continue to follow.
- As far as flowers for the table, I love peonies, so we put in a special peony garden, although sadly, their season is very short. But just as one type of flower is on its way out, another is on its way in, so it is always fresh and fun.

Maine Attraction

Jan and Ann ter Haar
Rose Cove, Maine

Jan ter Haar was not expecting to be enchanted by the Maine seacoast. In fact, when he suggested a coastal excursion to his wife, Ann, he was thinking more about checking an unvisited state off his bucket list and less about experiencing a life-changing encounter. The two rented a cottage for a summer, expecting to soak in the breezes and sea views. After one season spent experiencing the drama of watching the high seas, they sent out feelers to purchase a home of their own. After touring twenty-five houses, the couple found Rose Cove in 2007.

As a location, Rose Cove was everything they craved. Foremost, it overlooks a particularly scenic stretch of jagged shore where sailboats glide majestically past. Practically speaking, the house had stood empty for a year and a half prior to their occupancy. Not only did it beg for renovation, but also the house turned its back on the ocean, with no doors opening to the water and a floor plan that ignored the location. Wanting something much more outward facing, the couple mapped out changes to maximize the view, hired contractors, bought a bed and garden furniture, and "spent the first summer camping out in the house," ter Haar said, summing up their initial introduction to Maine homeownership. In truth, they loved every minute.

Ter Haar is Dutch, born with a strong vein of gardening in his blood, but Amsterdam could not satisfy his need to bond with the land or make it bloom. Rose Cove was full of potential. Because thirty-foot waves crashing on the rocks make wind an issue, previous owners had created a walled garden that is magical in its seclusion. The garden also serves to protect tender plants, vegetables, and fruit from the fury that can blow off the open water. However, the walled garden did not really relate to the majesty or magnitude of the location. And that is where Michael Walek came in.

Walek is a professional gardener who specializes in coastal properties and their unique opportunities. With the trained eye of a watercolor artist, he brings composition and color to the table. Case in point: He took one look at the walled garden and realized that it blocked any glimpse of the horizon. Although the surprise it offers is pure romance, he saw a way of adding to its allure by installing a corridor capped by a moon gate that frames the view.

Working with the garden's plantings, Walek's challenge was to thin out and update its contents with an emphasis on the espaliered fruit trees that thrive in that environment, which is a full zone warmer than the climate outside the walled confines. He also peppered flowers, herbs, and vegetables into the labyrinthine configuration. Asters, hydrangea cultivars, daisies, hellebores, phlox, Thalictrum, Pereskia, and Cimicifuga all share the alcoves with vegetables tossed in for continual harvest. Seating draws the couple to spend time within its protective walls.

Encased in climbing hydrangea, the walled garden is just a few steps from the house—easy for fetching homegrown produce for the kitchen. But beyond the moon gate is an open expanse where the ocean steals the show. Leading to the sea, a rill and pool

The view from the central axis of the garden frames the antique English birdhouse that Jan ter Haar repaints regularly to extend its lifespan.

take the axis outward and point toward the water. "The water features expand in size," Walek explains, "until finally you have the vastness of the ocean." Framed smartly in bluestone, the features add a geometric accent, leading the eye to a vermilion, pagoda-like birdhouse.

The house now sports both a screened porch/dining area and a terrace for lounging alfresco. Walek hemmed those spaces with beds of colorful annuals and perennials. Aware that the view is paramount, he left the sight lines open, with natural sculpture and windblown trees to anchor the foreground and direct the eye. Walek has studied what works and what does not fare so well when pitted against the extreme Maine environment, where the force of the wind sculpts the trees. In addition, inspired by Dutch garden designer Piet Oudolf, he is adding ornamental grasses to lend motion to the scene.

The garden continues to evolve as Walek and ter Haar work together to elevate it to new heights. More grasses are planned for the future, as are naturalistic plantings that echo the movement of the waves. Spaces are being simplified, while other plantings are in the process of maturing. Collaborating with the seacoast can be a challenge, but the partnership can also achieve pinnacles of beauty.

ABOVE: Gardner Michael Walek works in the walled garden, where a mature willow and cherry tree help shield it from the wind. On a clear day, boats scenically sail or speed by. OPPOSITE, TOP: Jan and Ann ter Haar enjoy the view down the main axis of the walled garden toward the ocean, framed in clouds of hydrangeas and Pereskia. BELOW: When Walek comes to work, he brings his dog along to patrol the corridor between the walled garden and the house. FOLLOWING SPREAD: The walled garden beside the house creates a microclimate that protects roses from the blustery winds off the shore, along with the rambling squash plant. Ter Haar finds buoys washed up on the shore and uses them as decoration.

WALEK'S POINTERS FOR A GARDEN BY THE SEA

- I have worked by the sea for decades, but every site presents its own set of parameters. Because Rose Cove is fully exposed, I began by bolstering the property's contingent of shrubs and trees to buffet the wind and provide framework.
- Junipers were a disappointment, browning where exposed to coastal winds. Given the property's name, roses seem like a no-brainer, but they have proved insufficiently hardy to tolerate the climate anywhere but in the walled garden.
- Working with flowering perennials can be dicey against the vast backdrop of the ocean. From a design standpoint, small plants with tiny flowers become swallowed up by the wide-open space. Statements must be broad, which prompted a ribbon of daylilies by the sea.
- Peonies of all types, Siberian iris, baptisia, Montauk daisies, and Aconitum are all success stories, while the plumes of ornamental grasses make a strong visual impact.
- Of course, plants that colonize to create a mass are always welcome. Where the view goes on forever, a sea of flowers feels like a natural.

Growing by Leaps and Bounds

Andrew Grossman
Seekonk, Massachusetts

The garden flows gracefully from one venue into the next. It swings fluidly from restive to energetic as you move through the space. If Andrew Grossman's garden feels deftly choreographed, it is no wonder. This landscape designer trained as a dancer, but he currently expresses movement with plants.

Although Grossman insists he "was not seriously looking for a property" when he saw the acre in Seekonk, Massachusetts, twenty years ago, it did not take much to convince him of its value. Certainly, he was not impressed by the dilapidated Cape Cod–style cottage or its array of garages circling around. If he was going to buy into land, he wanted more property than the single acre attached to the house. But then he caught an eyeful of the adjacent wildlife sanctuary stretching beyond the acre and realized that he would be getting a free view of majestic, unspoiled beauty. "The borrowed landscape sold me on the property," Grossman admits.

Botany was always in the back of Grossman's mind. Even when he was studying modern dance at Bennington College in Vermont, he gave classes in botanical science equal time. While his troupe was in London, he moonlighted helping maintain urban gardens. Upon returning to the States, he worked as a floral designer to supplement his performance earnings. And garden work helped pay his tuition when he returned to Bennington for a master's degree in choreography. In 1993, Grossman decided to pursue garden design professionally.

But first Grossman had to rescue the house. Originally, it was strangled in a nasty snarl of too many driveways and surplus garages. As soon as excess pavement was eliminated, he framed the cottage against a "hot garden" to jazz up the weathered shingles. Cresting the terrace on the house level, the color scheme is yellow, red, and orange. "It is the bright, vibrant Oz interlude," he says, referring to the combination of crocosmia, mandevilla, gladiolus, echinacea, daylilies, and Asiatic lilies.

Leaving generous pockets for annuals, Grossman finds that broad swaths of color—even vibrant color—are easy on the eye. "Masses are

Rudbeckia, Happy Face Yellow Potentilla, and California poppies combine with blue Adenophora, silver-leaf cytisus and 'Silver King' artemisia in landscape designer Andrew Grossman's garden.

more relaxing to look at," says the designer, who likes to group plants by color, not necessarily variety. "Massing creates tempo. Like movement, the hues are jumping up in the air." Meanwhile, the house received a lot of cosmetic surgery, going from pathetic to pleasing. For the landscape at the front entrance, Grossman embraced a cottage feeling, selecting pastels played out in lilacs, roses, honeysuckle, yarrow, foxgloves, peirevskia, and alchemilla. From there, he worked up the hill, adding a gazebo and another water lily pond.

All the disciplines of florist, designer, and dancer come into play in this garden of many moods. Grossman has applied thought and understanding to every twist and turn. It is an expertly choreographed performance that leaves one invigorated and always wanting more.

ABOVE: Grossman pauses beside a potted banana in his Seehonk garden. BELOW: Behind the house, Telekia speciosa (in the foreground) waves in a rivulet of yellow Lysimachia ciliata 'Firecracker,' and red Flower Carpet roses beside a checkerboard of thyme. OPPOSITE: A weathered arch marks the entrance to the flower garden. Filipendula, phlox, blue lobelia, and spring bulbs grow in the border. FOLLOWING SPREAD: Hyacinth bean, Eden roses, and honeysuckle climb the pergola, which serves as the entrance to the flower garden, where Grossman cultivates dwarf narcissus, English roses, dinnerplate dahlias, and cleome.

GROSSMAN'S
TIPS FOR A SUCCESSFUL FLOWER GARDEN

- Keep your plant variety selection to a minimum and plant them in large groupings.
- Figure out your color scheme. It will then limit your choices and make things easier to choose because a whole bunch of things are not available.
- Do not bite off more than you can chew. You do not know what the maintenance is going to look like for at least a year.
- I am not a huge fan of a long-term master plan. You might sell your house before the garden is finished. Focus on a one-to-three-year plan instead.
- Plants from the same family do not compete with each other. You can plant like plants really close together and get a full look faster.

ABOVE: Clematis montana 'Rubens' and Clematis 'Jackmanii' crown the gazebo with a clear view of a pond created to let Grossman experiment with the full spectrum of water lilies. On its banks, wisteria blossoms most of the summer. OPPOSITE, CLOCKWISE FROM TOP LEFT: Originally, Grossman planned to surround the garden with espaliered apple trees, but a vole invasion scuttled his plans. The rope and pillar fence was an elegant solution to his problem. A 'Royal Purple' smoke tree offsets 'Supreme Cantaloupe' Echinacea. In Grossman's garden, the last vestiges of a former driveway became a crescent-shaped gravel patio adjacent to the sunroom addition. A begonia-filled urn serves as a focal point amid layers of 'Snow Queen' hydrangea, Adenophora confuse, and hostas.

Stewardship Rediscovered

John Funt and Rick Childs
Norfolk, Connecticut

John Funt and Rick Childs knew they were fortunate to find one of the only flat fifty-plus acres of land in Norfolk, Connecticut, when they purchased High Meadows in 2002. Initially, the main draw was the serene and beautifully-proportioned 1917 Colonial Revival house, one of the later works of renowned architect Ehrick Rossiter. They set about creating a unified vision within the historic house. But soon the land began to speak to them, and they answered.

Both partners had busy schedules when the time came to address the landscape. Childs was an ER physician. Funt (the son of Allen Funt of *Candid Camera* fame) is a fine artist who refocused his career after working for Tiffany & Co. Both Childs and Funt are passionate gardeners: Childs is an avid (some might say obsessed) collector of conifers, while Funt takes a more diverse, artistic approach. Childs plotted the placement of conifers in dramatic spots as Funt dug, propagated, and coaxed a maximalist montage of flora out of the soil.

Originally, the pair planned to downsize in the horticultural arena. They figured that gardening would take a back seat. But the huge, level expanse with nothing but ancient pines toward the periphery felt empty without a garden. The space begged for the symmetry of a formal garden; it needed axes and cross-axes. And the challenge of balancing the scene against its open backdrop demanded certain dimensions. "It had to be an extension of the house," Funt explains. "The proportions just came to me." With a back terrace that stretches sixty feet wide, it was essential to go big.

Artist John Funt's garden's central axis features a heron wading in a pool. Noninvasive honeysuckle trained to crawl on a horizontal support provides a spark of color in a sea of green.

There were parameters: "It had to feel completely American," Funt says. "I was influenced by the classical American landscape architects and the location." The lack of a previous landscape allowed latitude for design without concern that they were treading on tradition. Funt found six matching fastigiate pin oaks to serve as sentinels. He also happened upon many magnolias, all sorts of conifers, and multiple lilacs to provide density. "But I am not a plant snob," he insists, offering his fondness for ivy, ajuga, nepeta, and violas as proof that he does not discriminate against more common plants.

What has evolved is a deeply soothing scene. The garden hums along in different shades of green with periodic accents supplied by flowering shrubs and perennial ground covers. Shapes and textures interweave to form a sophisticated blend. Funt admits that the garden was purposefully planted densely. "Some removals will be necessary," he says, "but that is understood." And he chose fast-growing shrubs and trees to make an immediate statement. Meanwhile, his training in art did more than help with conceptualization; it also furnished deeper lessons. "We have a visceral response to being here," Funt says. "This must have been something that was waiting to happen in our lives."

OPPOSITE: Funt created a dryscape for a side axis dominated by succulents, nepeta, Thermopsis, and a vintage mock orange. ABOVE: When he is not in the garden, Funt translates its bounty onto canvas in a barn converted into a studio.

BELOW: Metalwork by Stephen Bangs supports annual vines on the pergola. OPPOSITE, CLOCKWISE FROM TOP LEFT: Two Parrotia persica trees rise above a retaining wall. Funt combined a curbstone with a finial to create a chess-piece-like ornament. Childs's idea for dressing up a toolshed included dentil molding and quoins. A pair of Serbian spruces adorns the entrance drive. FOLLOWING SPREAD: A cauldron holding a shade-loving Astilbe accents a stone-encircled overlook.

FUNT'S APPROACH TO COLOR IN THE GARDEN

- When I refer to a pop of color, I do not necessarily mean something bright. One of my favorite plants is Viola 'Bowles' Black,' which has matte midnight petals so dark they almost slip into the shadows.
- Whether in my studio or in the gardens at High Meadows, I am always highly cognizant of color. Even when confined indoors due to weather, "I garden on my easel," he says of the landscapes he paints.
- Other ground covers also figure strongly in this landscape of overarching shades of green. Stonecrops (sedums) create carpets in varying degrees of red and orange foliage.
- I was once a ferocious shopper. Now I divide up plants to create color echoes. I feel like a pioneer spirit increasing and redistributing plants.
- In all my expressions, a lush sense of verdure prevails. Green is always the underlying theme.

The Devoted Gardener

Michael Devine
Orange, Virginia

Michael Devine and his partner, Thomas Burak, lived most of their adult lives in and around New York City. First, they had an apartment in Manhattan, then a house in Kinderhook in upstate New York. When Covid happened, they decided it was time to leave New York and set about looking for a house far from the fray where they could start a new chapter. After two years of searching for the right house, they stumbled upon a 1950s stone house in Orange, Virginia. The bucolic landscape and views of the Blue Ridge Mountains make the town of five thousand a desirable locale. The change of pace was a powerful draw for the two, who once had high-powered roles in New York—Devine with his fabric and tabletop designs, and Burak as creative director of Schumacher.

Designed by University of Virginia architecture professor Milton Grigg, the house stood amid a series of terraces carved into the hillside and offered the classic proportions of traditional design without the extreme maintenance associated with historic houses. Devine set about creating a series of gardens surrounding the house, separated by pretty old brick pathways. He is a hands-on gardener and does almost everything himself except tree work. "Thomas pitches in, too," says Devine, "but he is the reluctant gardener." The front of the house, being shaded, features a border of ferns and hydrangeas, much in the style of Gertrude Jekyll, who famously designed massive borders both deep and long. A pea gravel pathway

In the front of the house, a collection of large temple jars lines the wall, lending their year-round color to the facade. "Because the property is terraced, there are steps all over the gardens," says Michael Devine. A 'Madame Alfred Carrière' rose climbs the railing. It was a favorite of Virginian Nancy Lancaster.

is bordered by Russian sage, plumbago, celosia, and santolina.

Next is the "dry garden," a xeriscape that does not get watered and features plantings that can adapt to climate change. Species such as phlomis, verbascum, stachys, artemisias, lavender, and euphorbia thrive happily in the benign neglect. Devine got a hand from his neighbor Charlotte Moss for the lilac walk, which is underplanted with irises and peonies passed along from the designer. Also, in the style of Gertrude Jekyll, the walk is eighty feet long.

The cottage garden blooms with color and texture, with cosmos, celiosa, tagetes, hollyhocks, and roses. Devine happily putters among the flowers, snips blooms from the garden, and composes pretty arrangements to scatter around the house. Right off the kitchen, a stone terrace offers a convenient spot for outdoor dining. "We eat breakfast out there in nice weather," says Devine. "We also entertain out there. We can seat six in a pinch." The adjacent brick wall with arched doorways frames the dining table most picturesquely.

During the winter, Devine takes a break from his garden chores and plans for the next growing season. He gathers seeds from plants he deemed successful and starts them in his cold frame for the following spring. He also makes notes of plants he did not like such as the Lysimachia he planted a few years ago. "It went wild," he says. "It ran and ran all over the garden. I had to excavate it finally. It took two years to get rid of it." One would think that incident might have dampened his enthusiasm for the garden. But his tone as he describes the debacle leaves no doubt. He is loving every minute of it.

ABOVE, TOP RIGHT: Devine and partner, interior designer Thomas Burak, at the front door. RIGHT: The charming stone house with its classical details glows in the afternoon sun. OPPOSITE: A decorative, aged tuteur draws the eye to a bed of 'Orange Sunset' cosmos and 'Early Rose' celosia.

BELOW: Devine and Burak built the pretty stone and brick walls with wooden doors, which open onto the terrace where they like to entertain. OPPOSITE: Devine foraged his property for saplings to construct the wattle fencing in the garden. "I went to town with wattle," he says.

DEVINE ON HOW TO STEWARD AN INHERITED, ESTABLISHED GARDEN

- Wait a year to see what you have actually inherited.
- Think about cutting back overgrown, spindly plants. I had enormous rhododendrons in my yard, and I cut them back about a foot off the ground and they have grown back beautifully.
- If a plant is not doing well, do not despair. You can move it around until you find a spot where it is happy.
- Manage your woodland. We had a thick forest on our property and had a tree specialist come to thin out the trees. It has made a huge difference. It is like the trees can breathe again.
- I always tell Thomas, you can deadhead a plant or you can pick it and put it in a vase to enjoy. Also, the more you pick, the more blooms you will have.
- I strongly recommended trying your hand at seed sowing or propagation. Gardening is expensive enough without spending all your money at the garden shop.
- Share your riches. When you divide bulbs or take cuttings, pass some along to your pals. It is fun to see your gift blooming in a friend's garden.

Reflections in the Garden

India Hicks
Oxfordshire, England

A walk through the Grove's garden in Oxfordshire, England, would be a treat any time. But the opportunity to tour alongside India Hicks during her visit from her home in the Bahamas makes it even more special. The spirited designer, humanitarian, tastemaker, and goddaughter of King Charles III invariably adds a layer of anecdotal wit to any story, especially that of the country estate where she spent much of her childhood and where her mother, Lady Pamela, continues to live.

Dotted by sturdy stone churches, tidy cottages, and welcoming pubs, the countryside surrounding the Grove boasts history that dates back to Roman times. It was in the early 1960s that the area's solid country-squire lifestyle captured the fertile imagination of India's late father, David Hicks, the iconic interior designer and revolutionary in his field.

During our stroll, Hicks shares memories of her father. "He had a profound and lasting interest in the way people live," she says. "And he set the world on fire with his daring designs that other people were not doing." Throughout his halcyon years, as his design empire rapidly grew, David Hicks famously proclaimed that he was "undoubtedly the best-known interior designer in the world."

An impossibly handsome man, Hicks wore impeccable bespoke suits and oozed such panache that he seemed otherworldly. His disparate design projects included the White House bowling alley and a cocktail lounge on the *Queen Elizabeth II*, along with worldwide private commissions and several far-flung offices. That design prowess is also evident in his gardens at the Grove that unfold in a magical aura of symmetry with various intersecting "rooms" boasting a lush palette of his favorite shades of green.

While working on his plans for the essentially flat land, Hicks admitted that he had "always been attracted to gardens which have a great sense of containment." As he explained, "I feel the need for controlled, designed order. But what pleases me most is the true and totally disciplined sense of tonal gardening—green on green on green." This is particularly true in the Green Room, where he planted box bushes resembling rounded loaves of bread. Today, the space resounds with vast, mature vistas of massive hornbeam walls and avenues of Spanish chestnuts. This masterful roundup of verdancy delights the eye at different moments of the day when its composed impact is accompanied by delicate dewiness, flirting sunlight, or sweet birdsong.

Purposely removed from the linear garden, flowers were relegated to secret places because Hicks never wanted to see them from inside the house. All the while, he enjoyed the masterful crossover between his interior design mantras and his garden

An elegantly simple swimming pool tucked into an envelope of green offers summer refreshment.

fascinations, saying that "color means more to me than any of my other raw materials, and I often use strong colors together to make a dull corner sizzle." This is especially apparent in the Red Garden, which celebrates its namesake color with Copper beech walls and 'Danse du Feu' roses.

"The garden is a visible salutation to my father's imagination, as well as his high jinks," Hicks says. "He was precise, even down to the size of his ice cubes. But it is important to know that he saw the world differently. He was not like other friends' fathers who were bankers." Clearly amused by private memories, she laughs out loud as she adds, "He never read us bedtime stories, nor did he look at school reports. He wore capes lined in red satin and designed patent leather dancing shoes. He was a dreamer and an eccentric. We like eccentric."

ABOVE: An avenue of Spanish chestnut trees draws the eye toward the horizon. OPPOSITE, CLOCKWISE FROM TOP LEFT: India Hicks, attired in one of the romantic printed cotton dresses she usually wears in the country. A buttressed garden wall with climbing roses leads through a green tunnel to a door beyond. A weathered chalk-and-brick wall features a carved silhouette of Hicks's grandmother, Lady Edwina Mountbatten.

BELOW: The crenellated Gothick Pavilion includes carved finials, a retractable bridge, and a moat filled with lily pads. OPPOSITE: An expertly etched silhouette of debonair David Hicks, created by his artist son, Ashley, gazes from an unexpected corner of the garden. FOLLOWING SPREAD, LEFT, CLOCKWISE FROM TOP LEFT: With its overgrown grasses and tangles of pink climbing roses, a hidden corner of the garden offers a surprise from the otherwise manicured landscape. Hicks loved to punctuate a terminus for a path with a towering statue. A raised terrace is enlivened with wild lavender patches, an orb incised with David Hicks's signature monogram, and India's collection of cut roses for the house. A graceful, gothic-style door leads to a garden room lined with antique sculptures. OPPOSITE: David Hicks loved the sense of enclosure from walls created from trees and boxwoods punctuated by an urn.

HICKS'S TRIED-AND-TRUE ENTERTAINING TIPS

- Rely on your must-haves. Pretty napkins are mine. I do not mind whether it is a good linen napkin or a paper napkin, as long as they are pretty and clean. Set the table. It makes it feel that you have made the effort. I think something in the middle of the table is important.
- Adapt your table seasonally. My entertaining style changes by season. I always want a pretty table. I always love fresh flowers from the garden. I love to use old jam jars on an outdoor table. I do not want it to look pretentious.
- You can be a host anywhere. You do not have to live in the Bahamas. You do not have to have a beautiful garden in England. You can find a courtyard table at a swank resort and transform it by getting a new tablecloth, and by doing a huge arrangement of flowers.
- Cocktail hour is the most important meal of the day. It is the communing over a shared libation. It is the time that we stop, we pause, and we break bread together. We catch up with one another, we look each other in the eye, and we put our screens down.

Summer's Bounty

Zezé and Peggy O'Dea
Upstate New York

Year-round, floral designer Zezé creates spectacular arrangements for his A-list clientele in his Manhattan floral studio. But in the summer, the floral abundance ticks up a notch when his cutting garden in upstate New York comes into bloom. An acre of peonies, bearded irises, Oriental poppies, and delphiniums, chosen for their intense hues, anchors the farm and provides Zezé the materials for floral arrangements in the farmhouse. On Mondays, he loads a truck or two with flowers and takes them into the city for that week's orders. Zezé and his wife, Peggy O'Dea, spend their summer weekends at the farm, tending to the fifty-plus acres of landscape they have carved out of a scrappy plot. The reason you will not find the couple in the city on weekends has everything to do with the farm that feeds not only his shop but also his soul.

The farm meanders over the landscape between Hudson and Albany, populated by geese, ducks, cats, peacocks, chickens, and miniature donkeys. But its initial impression was anything but auspicious. "It was not that great," says Zezé. "Actually, it was very poor looking, but that is all we could afford." Over the years, the couple have added acreage and cleared brush to create impactful outdoor rooms meant for strolling. They have also added garden structures and focal points to the property—gazebos, statuary, and cupolas dot the landscape. During the commute back and forth to the city, Zezé and O'Dea often passed a derelict Lord & Burnham greenhouse. "The glass was broken," he says. "Trees were growing through the panes." They sought out the owner, adopted the greenhouse, and moved it to their property, where it now allows them to grow ferns, palms, and fuchsias that shower the floor with their blooms.

With his silent-movie-villain mustache, Zezé exudes an international flair. When he opened his shop almost fifty years ago in midtown Manhattan, he immediately caught the attention of the well-heeled clientele who adore his "more is more" sensibility. His success still suprises him. "As a commercial business I do everything wrong," he admits. "I am not open on Sundays, but our business is very successful." When the pair arrive at the weekend getaway, Zezé's first order of business is to swoop into the garden and cut flowers for bouquets he will scatter throughout the farmhouse. "I put flowers in the kitchen window. I put them on the dining room table. It makes all the difference."

The garden also supplies produce; kale, herbs, and vegetables for the couple's leisurely summer suppers. Zezé likes to work the textures of herbs and kale into his arrangements. "I try to put a little country in every bouquet," he says. A great sense of contentment prevails on the farm. "I am a happy person. I am never depressed. I look around my garden and think 'How fortunate we are.'"

Zezé and his wife, Peggy O'Dea, have been partners in business and in life for nearly fifty years. "We work well together," he says. The pair map out the orders for the week, O'Dea gathers the materials for each arrangement, and Zezé gets to work building the bouquets.

ABOVE: A customized gate in front of the rescued greenhouse keeps wandering fauna from feasting on the plants inside. OPPOSITE, CLOCKWISE FROM TOP LEFT: In the greenhouse, Zezé grows tropical plants that depend on the warmth. A dovecote gets plenty of visitors. FOLLOWING PAGES: A rustic bridge crosses the stream on the way to a gazebo the couple salvaged from a town square.

ZEZÉ'S APPROACH TO FLOWER ARRANGING

- I find delight in crafting a vibrant palette, embracing unexpected combinations. Hues of pink and orange, mingling with deep maroon, create a rich tapestry for the eye. The selection is careful. Not every blush of pink sings alongside every whisper of orange.
- I continuously seek uncommon flowers and foliage to distinguish each arrangement as something unique and memorable. Nature becomes my muse as I integrate vines and grasses into harmonious compositions.
- For those beginning their journey of floristry, I recommend using a vase with a subtle indentation. I reserve floral foam and frogs for moments of necessity, choosing instead to let the flowers find their own natural expression.
- Understanding the recipient of the arrangement informs my art. It allows me to weave the intention behind the card's message into a visual story told through blooms. Flowers, after all, should convey a heartfelt message.
- Music dances through our shop, conveying a serene ambience. I am drawn to the soothing notes of classical music and the gentle rhythms of bossa nova, each note harmonizing with the creativity at play.

BELOW: Peonies and irises were planted in rows for easy picking, while additional colors are continually added.
OPPOSITE, CLOCKWISE FROM TOP LEFT: A goose inspects a salvaged rustic bench. Zezé built the wattle fence and pergola.
An armillary sphere accents the herb garden. An antique cast-iron urn features cheeky cherubs.

Complex color combinations are key to floral designer Zezé's style. In a bouquet from his farm, he combines beauty bush, *Rosa glauca*, and honeysuckles with peonies and Oriental poppies.

GARDEN ELEMENTS

Every garden needs interest: a focal point, a conversation piece, something to attract and nurture birds, and bees, and butterflies, and humans—a place to hold flowers, vines, and shrubs, a place to rest or read or think, and to drink in the wonder in the sun or the shade, alone or with company.

Planters

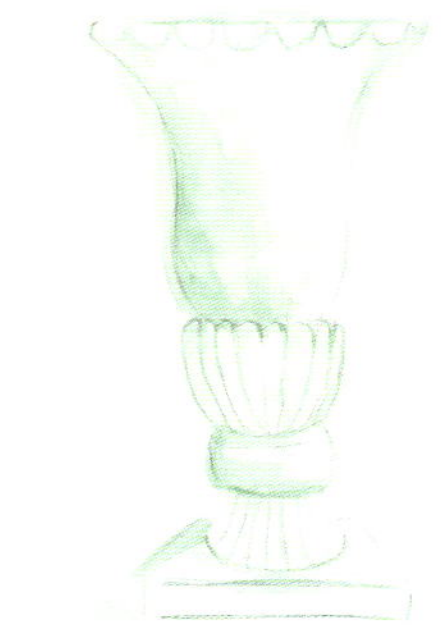

Planters are as much a part of the visual landscape as the plants chosen to live in them. There are as many styles, colors, materials, and designs as one can think of: the utilitarian, the modern, and the classic.

ABOVE, CLOCKWISE FROM TOP LEFT: A slate-colored rectangle holds a mix of plants in Fiona Tilley's rooftop West Village, Manhattan garden. These classic column-shaped planters in a graphite-colored composite material feature decorative architectural elements. A basket weave concrete planter was selected for a Fernando Wong project. Bettie Bearden Pardee favors cool and timeless green Caisse de Versailles planters. OPPOSITE: Weathered terra-cotta pots are effectively repeated along the old stone wall in David Hicks's English garden.

Classical shapes are a popular choice for planters. This well-loved patinated footed urn is a prime example.

ABOVE: An aged painted terra-cotta urn holds a humble cluster of anemones, muscari, hyacinths, and ferns. OPPOSITE, CLOCKWISE FROM TOP LEFT: These contemporary mottled concrete planters can also serve as mini-gardens, and the repetition is an interesting visual element. An antique, footed urn in a deep terra-cotta color with bas relief is a nice contrast to the spikey modern planting. Inverted pyramid-shaped planters on solid square bases lend themselves to more graphic, spikey plants, especially those that do not drape, which allows for the full shape of the planter to be seen. French gardens are often filled with more utilitarian planters like these galvanized metal buckets. The more neutral silver bases nicely set off the lush reds of the blooms.

Statuary

Art in the outdoors plays several roles. It can be a finishing touch in a landscape, create a point of interest, convey a message, provide a visual pause, or just interrupt an expanse.

ABOVE, CLOCKWISE FROM TOP LEFT: A casting of a sailboat-shaped dial tells time in this sundial birdbath in Nantucket. Pineapples, first appearing in America in the seventeenth century, were rare and exotic. They became a symbol of hospitality and remain so to this day—here, as finials welcoming visitors into a Nantucket garden. An urn perched on a pedestal lends a moment of drama at the rise of this allée on the estate of Chatsworth in Derbyshire, England. This stately lion at Ditchley Park, in Oxfordshire, England, is a prime example of concrete animal statuary seen throughout the great estates of Europe. OPPOSITE: Landscape architect John Howard chose this oversized Italian olive jar sculpture as a focal point for a pool and garden in Atlanta.

ABOVE: Armillary are a popular garden feature and are often used in the center of a hardscaped area or greensward. Here, an armillary on a pedestal in this Little Compton, Rhode Island garden, is an impactful counterpoint to the hedges and soft white blooms. OPPOSITE: "Falling Leaf," created by David Harber and the David Harber Guild, is a graceful 11.5-foot-tall bronze interpretation of a leaf that gives the illusion of falling into the water in this installation garden at the Chelsea Flower Show.

ABOVE: Torus, David Harber's modern sculpture in polished stainless steel, reflects the environment wherever it lives. It's a bold but whimsical garden element. OPPOSITE, CLOCKWISE FROM TOP LEFT: A bust of the goddess Athena nestles into branches in the garden at Plantsville Pines, a lush Connecticut property. Gardens are wonderful opportunities for playfulness and imagination to hold sway. Rusted bird sculptures have been set, cheekily, atop a rusted sundial in the garden at Plantsville Pines. Statuary can add emotion and movement to an outdoor space, like this contemporary statue of a woman embracing the day in a Newport, Rhode Island garden. An antique olive jar, overgrown with ivy, gives this space a sense of time passing and the garden having its way at Kelmarsh Hall in Northampton, England.

Architecture

Outdoor spaces throughout garden history have been graced with all manner of architecture: follies; pergolas; arches; walls; pavilions; pagodas; temples to gods of nature; even playhouses for the children of the house. It's those contributions made by human hands that add a personal point of view to the property.

ABOVE: Treillage and a bamboo gazebo support climbing vegetables in this magical potager created by the late garden writer and gardener Jack Staub at Hortulus Farm in Bucks County, Pennsylvania. OPPOSITE: New "ruins" and a cheerful yellow Chinese Chippendale bridge, conceived by garden designers Isabel and Julian Bannerman, draw attention and imagination to this secluded spot at Woolbeding Gardens in Sussex, England.

ABOVE: Garden designer and plantsman Renny Reynolds built this charming pavilion from a kit. With its sweeping views of the golf course and tropical plantings, it is a much-loved setting for brunches, lunches, and dinners. OPPOSITE, CLOCKWISE FROM TOP LEFT: Designer Charlotte Moss's East Hampton garden wall features a rich, sky blue-painted moon gate. Swift River Farm in Massachussetts boasts a wood and shingle gazebo tucked into perennial blooms and boxwoods. It plays host to weekly dinners and garden gazers. Climbing roses have found a safe home on this treillage on the side of a cedar shake cottage in Nantucket. One of eight Victorian glass houses glistens amid the clipped hedges and topiaries in the garden at Eythrope, in Buckinghamshire, England.

ABOVE: This fanciful replica of an English thatch-roofed cottage was a tenth birthday gift for Peggie Phipps, daughter of the family who built Old Westbury, the iconic early twentieth-century Long Island estate. OPPOSITE: Tucked into a private garden, this Greek Revival-style temple makes for an inviting spot for repose.

The crisp, white treillage on this outbuilding adds to the glamour of a grass tennis court at Liz Lange's East Hampton house, Grey Gardens.

Living Sculpture

Shaping plants has been around since ancient Rome, where the word "topiarius" in Latin means ornamental gardener. From chess men to a checkerboard, with arches and espaliers in between, the playful use of plants makes for clever, whimsical moments in the outdoors.

ABOVE: The topiary chess garden at Haseley Court, last residence of American gardener and decorator Nancy Lancaster was planted in 1850, and thrives to this day, thanks to the loving care of each successive owner. OPPOSITE: Dutch garden designer Piet Oudolf created this tunnel of beech and Cornelian cherry that connects his farmhouse lawn to the driveway.

ABOVE: The no-drama antique rambler rose, 'Super Excelsa' climbs and clings to the archways at Plantsville Pines in Connecticut. OPPOSITE, CLOCKWISE FROM TOP LEFT: Landscape designer Fernando Wong trained Confederate jasmine in a geometric design to define the pool area of this Palm Beach, Florida home. A thyme checkerboard garden creates a playful point of interest in the garden of this Seekonk, Massachusetts property. A hedged circular parterre garden adds a bit of fancy and structure to a rustic setting in the garden at Beanacre Farm in Fairfield, Connecticut. Interior designer and avid gardener Bunny Williams plants a parterre garden outside her conservatory starting with tulips. She switches up floral plantings seasonally.

Furniture

In order to be still enough to truly experience the magic of outdoors, one needs places to perch—benches, chaises longues, and chairs of every shape, size, style, color, and material. They become as much a part of the space as the growing things.

ABOVE, CLOCKWISE FROM TOP LEFT: In Kate Brodsky's East Hampton garden, frothy white hydrangeas find a place to rest on an antique garden bench. This traditional wrought-iron outdoor chair on a Mount Airy, Pennsylvania, porch gets a fun and graphic update covered in an exaggerated leaf-patterned fabric. Wendy Wurtzburger, the homeowner, is a design and retail visionary. Garden designer Piet Oudolf unwinds in these vivid orange/red outdoor armchairs. "This is my favorite place if I want to relax," he says of the chairs in front of his studio. Garden designer Renny Reynolds and the late Jack Staub painted these wrought-iron ice-cream chairs a perky pale blue to add color and whimsy to this private spot in the gardens of Hortulus Farm in Bucks County, Pennsylvania. OPPOSITE: An antique wrought-iron bench in cream nestled between fern-filled urns at the end of a gravel path, is the perfect destination after a stroll in Bettie Beardon Pardee's Newport garden.

ABOVE: Dallas-based landscape architect Melissa Gerstle reflects the spirit of the place in her Kips Bay pool and patio space. The sleek black coffee tables and draped daybeds bring a drama that one expects for Dallas, but the neutral palette and flowy fabric drop the temperature. OPPOSITE: The late Nancy Lancaster, legendary Virginia decorator and gardener, designed this spider web garden bench for her property at Haseley Court, in Oxfordshire, England. Placed at the end of the laburnum allée, it is a visual exclamation point that adds an unexpected, exotic seating opportunity.

ABOVE: Poppy red metal outdoor chairs with a hard-working wood dining table overlook a colorful wildflower meadow in New York's Hudson Valley. OPPOSITE, CLOCKWISE FROM TOP LEFT: Sharon Santoni's French country garden in Normandy is a dreamy, flower-filled world where dogs and people ramble and take in the beauty. Simple white bistro chairs and table provide a place to pause. This oversized lounge chair with its soft contours makes for a cozy contrast to the split-face coral wall backdrop in a Jupiter Island, Florida-area, by landscape designer Keith Williams. A garden niche and wall draped in purple clematis vine featuring a weathered stone bench is one of Plantsville Pine's hidden gems. North Carolina interior designer Francie Hargrove makes this porch as comfortable and inviting as the interior with performance fabric slip-covered seating, area lighting, fabric panels to frame the opening, and a warm wooden table.

ARRANGEMENTS

Flowering the out of doors, whether for parties or planters, requires a deft use of color, strategic plant material selection, an understanding of scale and proportion, and most important of all, beauty. We're presuming to improve upon the landscape in some ways, and that involves true artistry. One of the most intriguing and intentional styles of arranging is to forage, at least some items, from the garden. It is the most sustainable style and marries the decorated surfaces with the surroundings.

A Container for the Senses

James Farmer
Perry, Georgia

Garden-to-table lifestyle guru James Farmer creates a verdant arrangement that he plants for summer get-togethers and then later repurposes in the garden.

Farmer's inspiration for this container arrangement was a mélange of textures and tones found on the planter proper as well as the plants themselves. He loves a container for the senses—a composition that looks, feels, smells, and tastes wonderful. It can even sound wonderful, too, with just the right rustling of leaves. He has a weakness for planters, pots, urns, and jardinières with flaky paint and rusty facades. It's that perfect mix of high and low styles—an earthy surface melded with the container's good design. Engaging the other senses thus becomes paramount to balance the visual delight.

Chartreuse, silvery white, sage, and jade are found within the plants he chose and in some of the grain of the urn itself. It is a harmony of these shades that thrills him.

ABOVE: James Farmer at his home in Perry, Georgia. RIGHT: The finished product, a rustic planter filled with plants of all different colors, textures, shapes, and scents.

1

MATERIALS

- sphagnum moss
- Cuban oregano
- 'Provence' Lavender
- 'Angelina' sedum
- Greek columnar basil
- curly leaf parsley
- Dusty Miller
- orange mint

2

TOOLS & SUPPLIES

- antique cast-iron urn
- terra-cotta shards
- my "Farmer's mix" planting medium (finely ground pine bark, sphagnum moss, mushroom compost or manure compost, and a built-in time-release fertilizer)
- long, narrow-spouted watering can

3 Layer the bottom of the planter with terra-cotta shards. This prevents water from running out too fast from the drainage hole and keeps the potting soil from seeping out. Gravel or wire mesh work well too.

4 Fill the container about half full with potting soil. Tamp it down to provide a sturdy base for plants to begin their growth. Planted compositions such as these are intended for instant gratification and can serve as temporary centerpieces before being repurposed throughout the garden.

5 Break up, massage, and score the root ball before planting, as shown here with the Cuban oregano. In a tight planting situation, breaking up the excess soil allows for more planting room. Plus, this stimulates the roots for growth.

6 Start with your larger plants and fill in with your smaller specimens. I'm always reminded of a children's choir at church—arrange the taller kids in the back and the shorter kids up front. Here, the taller plant, Greek columnar basil, acts as a sentinel for the anchor plant, Cuban oregano. Then add the 'Angelina' sedum around the base.

7 No two leaves and no two plants are identical. The narrow leaves of the 'Provence' lavender are a lovely complement to the wider, rounder leaves of the Cuban oregano. Now that shape contrast is underway, interject color contrast. Enter Dusty Miller. This silvery gray-green is a sharp contrast to the purer green oregano and basil, but the lavender is a good middle hue.

8 Sometimes a plant is really several individual plants growing together. I often split plants, such as this orange mint, to increase the volume of my plant material and give me slender specimens.

9 In kindergarten I was reprimanded for eating a green crayon. "I wanted to taste the color green," was my defense. Parsley is my panacea for planters, for it's a green I can eat any time! Here it fills in space and spills over the edge of the urn.

Fruits and Flowers

Canaan Marshall
Atlanta, Georgia

Canaan Marshall, Atlanta-based floral and event designer, brings a festive rainbow of fruits and flowers to a poolside luncheon in Atlanta. His directive to lay floral arrangers regarding party flowers: "Choose flowers you like; put some love into the preparation and have fun."

ABOVE, CLOCKWISE FROM TOP: Lanterns, grasses, and luscious mixed arrangements set the stage for a spectacular summer dinner. Canaan didn't want anyone at the pool to be without flowers, so he conceived mixed arrangements that mimic the ones on the table to sit next to each chaise longue. A close-up of one of the designs between the chaises. The mix of blooms is held by an aged terra-cotta pot. OPPOSITE, LEFT TO RIGHT: The designer at work on a floral creation. A detail of the table scape, including aqua-toned place settings and glassware and a profusion of summer-colored roses, lilies, and fruits including berries

Light and Airy

Sybil Sylvester
Birmingham, Alabama

For an autumn alfresco dinner party at Margot and Gates Shaw's home in Birmingham, Alabama, floral design specialist Sybil Sylvester pulled her palette for the arrangements from the Lee Jofa floral-patterned fabric on the tablecloths. "The magic is in the details," she shares. "I love the way the flowers dance and echo the blooms in the table linens." Sylvester kept the arrangements low enough for cross-table conversation to happen easily.

ABOVE, CLOCKWISE FROM TOP: Lights and flowers repeated down the harvest table made a strong visual impression. A detail of the place setting with the colorful floral and botanical linens illustrates the inspiration for floral designer Sybil Sylvester's palette. Sybil Sylvester. OPPOSITE, LEFT: Hosts, Margot and Gates Shaw. RIGHT: For the centerpieces, Sylvester chose a mix of colors, shapes, and heights, and placed them in galvanized tin troughs for a rustic feel for this alfresco supper.

Acknowledgments

While I have continued to travel the country speaking on behalf of *Flower* magazine and have continued to sell and sign copies of my first book, *Living Floral*, it became obvious to me a while back that there was a need for a sequel—to carry on the story, to take it outside, if you will. But life remains full and busy, and I let the call drop—until a dinner at the American Horticulture Society's River Farm in a tent one stormy night.

I had the good fortune of sitting near Rizzoli Publisher Charles Miers. Toward the end of our conversation he mentioned that my book had done very well, and that I should consider another one. I hastily and enthusiastically responded that I would love it, especially if my stellar editor on the first book, Sandy Gilbert Freidus, could tackle my sophomore effort. She has.

I knew with all that the magazine world entails, I would need help with writing and imagining the book, so I went back to the *Living Floral* well and invited Lydia Somerville to reprise her original role. She has.

With a pattern beginning to unfold, I asked Ellen Padgett, *Flower*'s art director who designed the first book, to return to the drawing board to design this book. She has.

It is with profound thanksgiving that I acknowledge Karen Carroll. Karen has been a constant friend, support, mentor (though much younger than I), adviser, and fixture in *Flower* land—taking on different roles as the magazine's need and the opportunities in her life arose. But it is her most recent title of editorial director that has made my undertaking of this project possible. With her unerring eye and pitch-perfect ear, her fearless yet always humble confidence in guiding me and the content of the magazine, Karen has enabled me to rest assured it is in safe hands while I tended to the work of this book.

I also want to thank all of team *Flower*, who passionately and tirelessly work together to create magic: Nicole Bowman, Jason Burnett, Kate Chapman, Carrie Clay, Suzanne Cooper, Julie Doll, Julie Durkee, Wendy Ellis, Steven Fisher, Amanda Smith Fowler, Julie Gillis, Mercy Lloyd, Marlee Mims, Jennel O'Brien, Ellen Padgett, Sara Taylor, and Patrick Toomey.

This book is filled with beautiful outdoor places and the people who dwell, garden, and entertain in them. I am so grateful to all those who opened their worlds to us and shared the beauty and their personal perspectives.

Photography Credits

Stacy Bass: page 205 (bottom right)

Bryan Bieder: page 188

Carmel Brantley: pages 83–89, 183 (bottom right), 205 (top left)

Monica Buck: page 196

Jonathan Buckley/Bloomsbury Publishing: page 186 (bottom left)

Sabine Bungert/Living Inside: pages 202, 207 (bottom right)

Rob Cardillo: pages 171–179, 195, 207 (bottom left)

Claudine Casbarian for Julie Soefer Photography: pages 53–59

Courtesy of Chatsworth Estate: page 189 (bottom right)

Kindra Clineff: pages 22–27, 107–115, 135–139, 141–147, 184–185, 186 (top right and bottom right), 189 (top left and right), 190, 192 (top left, right, and bottom right), 197 (top and bottom right), 204, 205 (top right), 210 (top left and bottom right), 211

Alison Conklin: page 207 (top right)

Paul Costello: pages 77–81

Mary Craven Dawkins: front cover, pages 37–43

Emily Followill: page 210 (bottom left)

James Gillispie: page 8

Tria Giovan: pages 15–21, 69–75, 183 (top left), 207 (top left)

Mick Hales: pages 2, 117–125, 183 (bottom left), 205 (bottom left), 206, back cover

David Harber: page 193

Tom Hatton: page 197 (bottom left)

David Hillegas: pages 6, 11, 91–97, 99–103, 187, 216–219

Stephen Karlisch: page 208

Gavin Kingcome: page 191

Erik Kvalsvik: pages 61–67, 156–161

Marianne Majerus: pages 194, 198

Charlotte Moss: pages 189 (bottom left), 192 (bottom left), 203, 209, 223

Michael Mundy: pages 5, 127–133, 197 (top left), 199, 200, 221

Clive Nichols: pages 163–169, 182

Courtesy of Pennoyer Newman: page 182

Caroline Petters: pages 214–215

Brooke Slezak: pages 29–35

Michael Starvaridis: pages 186 (top left), 210 (top right)

Shelly Strazis: pages 44–51

Claire Takacs: pages 148–155

ILLUSTRATION CREDITS
Marlee Ledbetter Mims: pages 182, 188, 194, 202, 206

PAGE 2: A quiet moment in Bettie Bearden Pardee's Newport, Rhode Island, garden.

PAGE 5: A blue gate at Grey Gardens, East Hampton, New York.

PAGE 6: An alfresco tableau at Brierfield—Margot and Gates Shaw's Alabama farm.

PAGE 221: Designer Thomas O'Brien's parterre garden in Bellport, New York

PAGE 221: Climbing ivy and flowers at Nancy Lancaster's Haseley Court in Oxfordshire, England.

ENDPAPERS: Taplow fabric and wallpaper by Lee Jofa.

SECTION OPENERS: Althea fabric and wallpaper by Lee Jofa.

First published in the United States of America in 2026
by Rizzoli International Publications, Inc.
49 West 27th Street
New York, NY 10001
www.rizzoliusa.com

Publisher: Charles Miers
Editor: Sandra Gilbert Freidus
Art Direction: Ellen Shanks Padgett
Production Manager: Rebecca Ambrose
Editorial Coordination: Kelli Rae Patton and Sara Pozefsky
Managing Editor: Lynn Scrabis

ISBN: 978-0-8478-7630-3
Library of Congress Control Number: 2025943318

Printed in China
2026 2027 2028 2029/10 9 8 7 6 5 4 3 2 1

The authorized representative in the EU for product safety and compliance is Mondadori Libri S.p.A., via Gian Battista Vico 42, Milan, Italy, 20123, www.mondadori.it

Visit us online:
Instagram.com/RizzoliBooks
Facebook.com/RizzoliNewYork
Youtube.com/user/RizzoliNY